Nursing Your Horse

NURSING YOUR HORSE

Diana R. Tuke

The Crowood Press

First published in 1999 by
The Crowood Press Ltd
Ramsbury, Marlborough
Wiltshire SN8 2HR

British Library Cataloguing in Publication Data

A catalogue record for this book is available from the British Library.

ISBN 1 86126 272 8

All photographs by Diana Tuke except: page 10, John Evetts; page 125, Listers; and pages 15, 22,
23, 29 (top), 45, 52, 53, 57, 59 (bottom), Donald Tuke.

Line-drawings by Sara Wyche, except those on pages 28, 44, 54, 73, 76, and 122, which are by
Elizabeth Mallard-Shaw.

Edited and designed by OutHouse Publishing Services
Printed in Great Britain by WBC Book Manufacturers Ltd, Mid Glamorgan

Contents

Acknowledgements—

Without all the help that I have received over the years, I would never have learnt to care for my horses and ponies following all the injuries and illnesses that have cropped up at various times since the last war. Nor would I have had the courage to fight back and ultimately recover from my own injuries. With the help and support of my family, the Dulverton (East) Hunt, the Beaufort Hunt, and Olympic riders of the 1960s and 1970s, I returned to hunting, showing and eventing, and in consequence had my own horses who would provide some of the information for *Nursing Your Horse*! My grateful thanks goes to them all.

I would also thank the veterinary surgeons who have attended my horses over the years, and the people, firms and associations whose co-operation has been invaluable during the writing of this book. These include Animalcare Ltd, who supplied information on Identichips; Animal Health Trust, who supplied the photograph of the scanning; the Welfare Department of the British Horse Society, who provided some of the information on poisonous plants and other welfare issues; Challenger Distribution Ltd, for their help with new products; Clayton Equestrian Safety, who gave advice; Equest, who supplied information on the new moxidectin wormer; Equestrian Security Services, who supplied information and allowed me to photograph the freeze-branding of River Gipsy; Chris Hale of MSD AGVET, a division of Merck, Sharp and Dohme Ltd, who gave information on worming horses and ponies and provided the photograph of Eqvalan; Robinson Animal Healthcare, who provided advice on Animalintex and the new Flexus bandage; Stockshop-Wolseley Ltd., for Miss Nathalie Andre's help and for supplying the Wolseley Skylark clippers used to keep hair short when treating injuries.

I am grateful to Mr Dovedale MRCVS of Greenwood, Ellis & Partners MsRCVS, who very kindly allowed me to photograph the process when he came to X-ray River Gipsy's off-hind fetlock; and to River Gipsy's veterinary surgeons, Mercer & Hughes MsRCVS , and to Mr Peter Hughes MRCVS, for all they did for River Gipsy in the last few years and for allowing me to photograph her having an injection; to Paul I'anson, who let me photograph River Gipsy's dental treatment; to Mr H.R. Feilden BVSc MRCVS of Solvery-Dupher Veterinary for help with the vaccination section of the book; to Mr Tim Greet MRCVS, of Rossdale & Partners, who removed the wolf tooth embedded in River Gipsy's lower jaw, making her happy again; and to Miss Isobel Prestwich, River Gipsy's chiropractor who kindly permitted me to photograph her working;

I am indebted to Mrs Georgina Kirkland and her family, who so generously allowed River Gipsy to take up residence in their stables in 1991. This meant that I was able to keep her to the end, which would otherwise have been impossible because my father was very ill and I would not have been able to cope. Also to Mrs

ACKNOWLEDGEMENTS

Susanne Reich and her horse Midday Phlight for allowing his photograph to be used on the cover, and my brother Lt.-Com. Donald Tuke RN for doing some of the photography.

Finally, a very special thank you to all the horses and ponies, who have taught me so much over the years: Witchery, Jackie, Points, Castania, Loyal Toast, Canyon, Willow Moth, Galavant, and Galavant's daughter, River Gipsy; and, in addition to my own equine friends, all those horses and ponies that I have met over the years and helped to nurse back from illness or injury. Rewarding work.

Introduction ──────────────────

Every owner, at some time or another, will be faced with having to nurse a horse or pony through illness or injury. The problem may be of a minor nature, or it may be very serious, but in either case the quality of care that the horse receives will have a considerable effect on the speed of his recovery.

Cases of minor injury or mild illness can often be treated without the assistance of a vet, and provided you can see a positive response to your treatment within a couple of days there should be no need to call for professional help; if on the other hand your treatment does not appear to be having much effect within this time you should not hesitate to call your veterinary surgery. The complexity and severity of the condition will determine how soon to call the vet, but if you are in the slightest doubt you should call for help immediately. This is important not only for your horse's welfare, but for the purposes of making a claim on your insurance. (And any owner who does not have insurance may well come to regret it.)

Few owners are lucky enough never to have an ailing or injured horse or pony in their care. Some owners imagine they are among this fortunate few because they do not realize that their equine friend is ill or injured, and requires careful nursing and, possibly, veterinary treatment. Other owners are aware that there is something wrong but simply do not want to bother nursing – however serious the case may be. The first of these three groups are indeed lucky; the middle group merely need help and encouragement to do what is right by their horse or pony; the latter group have no right to own or care for any horse, pony or donkey, or for that matter, any kind of animal.

Incidentally, though this book is about horses and ponies, donkeys and mules are generally included. However, if you do own one, it may wise in each individual case to check with your veterinary surgeon that there are no differences in treatment.

Nursing is a time-consuming business, but good nursing is absolutely essential if full and satisfactory recovery is to be achieved. Although Mother Nature is a good healer, and time is said to heal all wounds, the results may not be as satisfactory as they are in patients that are given proper care. In many cases good nursing can mean the difference between life and death, a return to work or loss of use. Nevertheless, there are some cases, however hard one fights, however long hours one spends, where saving the animal is impossible. It either has to be put down to save further pain and distress, or else will drop dead before the veterinary surgeon can administer treatment. These cases are of course devastating, although there is at least some consolation in knowing that the animal is at peace and not left in terrible pain. One can come to terms with it, but it takes time. Over the years I have had my fair share of accidents, illness and injuries; but I have also bought 'rescue' cases to put right. Giving a second chance to a horse that seems to be a hopeless case is rewarding work.

In action: the author with Galavant, Stowell Park, Gloucestershire, April 1972.

In *Nursing Your Horse*, I hope to help owners and others looking after horses and ponies, to achieve the best possible results, and return their charges to work within the minimum time. Some cases, though, will require a lot of time, and that time must be given. However much you yourself might wish to use the horse or pony, you must resist any temptation to do so as you will subject the patient to further pain and distress, which will result in a far longer convalescence, or permanent loss of use, or, worse still, loss of the patient.

In no way is *Nursing Your Horse* intended to cover ever problem that may beset our horses and ponies, nor is it in any way designed to be used in place of professional help and advice. Rather it is intended as a guide to the ways you can help to make veterinary treatment more effective – and significantly enhance your horse's prospects of recovery – through sound nursing and conscientious care.

It is amazing what can be achieved if one is prepared to give up the time to nurse properly. In the end it is worth every second, for to have a horse satisfactorily return to work when no one thought it possible is something one never forgets.

1 Principles of Sound Nursing ———

Horses and ponies are like very young children in that they cannot tell you what is wrong with them. You have to find out, and then persuade them to let you help them get better – which is not always easy. Observation is the key; and if you can watch them

1. muzzle
2. chin
3. angle of jaw
4. bridge of nose
5. jowl
6. poll
7. neck
8. crest
9. point of shoulder
10. withers
11. back
12. loins
13. point of hip
14. croup
15. dock
16. thigh
17. gaskin
18. hamstring
19. point of hock
20. stifle
21. hindquarters
22. ribs
23. point of elbow
24. shoulder
25. jugular groove
26. forearm
27. flank
28. knee
29. cannon bone
30. fetlock
31. coronet
32. pastern
33. bulb of heel

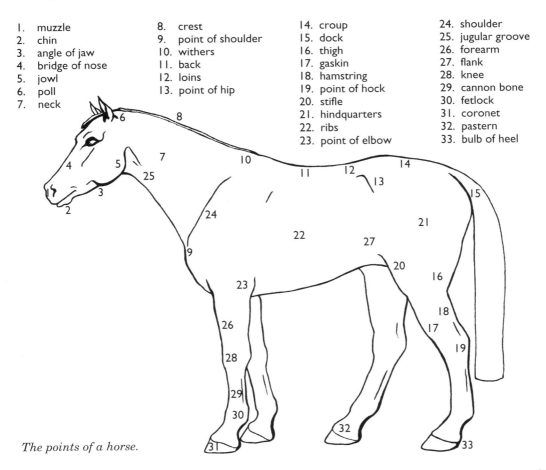

The points of a horse.

without their realizing you are there, so much the better for you will be able to make a far more objective assessment of progress.

First and foremost you must overcome your horse's fear, and the distrust that naturally accompanies pain. Once you have gained your patient's confidence you will find that half the battle is won. The rest is down to considerate nursing and common sense. If your veterinary surgeon is involved, then do listen and follow his instructions, and do keep him informed of progress. If the condition deteriorates, you should of course contact the vet as soon as possible; but do not phone your surgery out of hours in cases that do not necessitate attention until working hours the next day.

In some cases, it can seem a long time before you start to see the results of your endeavours. This may be frustrating, but it is important to be patient and not to take shortcuts.

There are three basic principles of sound nursing:

- Cleanliness.
- Concientiousness.
- Consideration.

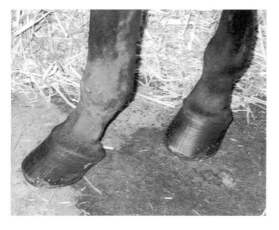

The hind fetlock clipped, and the floor swept clean, prior to treatment. River Gipsy, July 1993.

CLEANLINESS

The standard of hygiene observed while nursing can have a significant effect on the results of your endeavours. The importance of cleanliness applies to the equipment, the handler, the treatment, and to the stables themselves. Everything must be kept spotless. Stables, tools, buckets, rugs, grooming kits, hay nets – all items around the horse or pony – must be kept clean and disinfected. The horse himself also needs to be kept clean. Any dirty patches on the body will need to be brushed or carefully washed off with warm water to which a few drops of liquid antiseptic has been added. All buckets and sponges should be disinfected before and after use.

Making sure that this high standard of hygiene is maintained may sometimes seem laborious, but it should not be neglected because it is essential in order to stop the spread of infection.

I remember a few years ago at a livery yard, the owner was away and had inadvertently taken the bulk of the veterinary cupboard with her. In her absence one horse out at grass caught himself up on a hurdle with a sharp base, cutting himself badly. While waiting for the attention of the vet, the injured horse's leg was bandaged. A veterinary surgeon

- Wear gloves to protect your hands and to prevent infection. I find the PVC ones work well for general duties, but disposable or surgical gloves are better for more close-contact work, such as wound dressing.

- If you do not wear gloves make sure that your hands and nails are thoroughly scrubbed before and after treatment, or when cleaning materials in contact with the patient. This may seem very fussy but it is worth while and only sensible.

was eventually able to get to the yard; and I offered to scrub and disinfect a bucket for him, as I had some antiseptic of my own. But he waved it away – a little dirt didn't matter! He removed the temporary bandage, and managed more or less to clean the wound off – cotton wool had been used and stuck to the deep wound, but with most of the first-aid kit missing there had been nothing else to try to stop the bleeding. The horse was frantic with pain, and in his panic caused the dressing to be dropped on filthy ground. To my amazement, it was shaken to remove the dirt and then applied. I was horrified, and thankful that the patient was not my horse.

In this case, the cut healed but it took a long time. Had it been really clean it would have healed sooner. There are doubtless many occasions when the basic rules of hygiene are flouted in this way. But it is never worth it in the long run.

CONSCIENTIOUSNESS

This basically means putting your patient first. It may be time consuming and exhausting, especially if you are working as well.

Galavant nearly lost River Gipsy as a foal. I found her discharging early one morning when I went to feed her. By being kept quiet, she made it through the day; but from then on, until she foaled two months later, I checked her regularly day and night. Supervision is vital in both minor and serious cases, round the clock if the case is very serious.

Attention to detail is essential. Even apparently trivial oversights can have

Attention to detail is the hallmark of good nursing, and it should extend even to the management of the muck heap. River Gipsy enjoying the snow in March 1995.

13

long-term effects. Make sure you understand instructions from your vet, and follow them precisely, and use your common sense to ensure that you are doing things correctly.

Keep records of progress: use a notebook and after each treatment write down the details of what has been given and how the patient responded. Keep the notebook handy for your own reference and to provide the basis of progress reports to the vet.

Monitor your horse's temperature (*see* Chapter 5). Take the patient's temperature morning and night to check that it is remaining stable. If the temperature rises, take it more frequently. Keep a record of the time and the reading each time it is taken.

CONSIDERATION

Use your imagination to help you see what your patient needs, and make the necessary effort to keep him comfortable. A horse that is peaceful and contented will recover far quicker than one who is stressed or uncomfortable.

Medicines

- Medicines must be administered at the correct times. This is especially important for drugs such as antibiotics, which need to be given at regular intervals and the course fully completed if they are to be effective.

- All drugs need to be dealt with carefully and administered in accordance with veterinary instructions. Proper care must be taken to ensure that rules of hygiene are observed.

- Store drugs securely, out of reach from children and other animals, and at the correct temperature (some have to be kept cold and others at room temperature). Always check the storage instructions on the container.

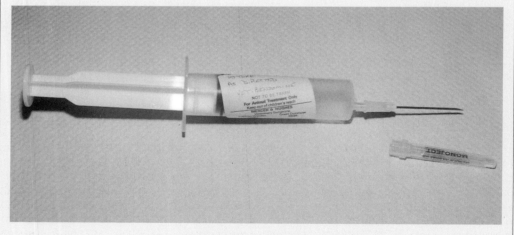

The owner may be given substances like antibiotics for the continuation of an injection course. The syringe should be clearly labelled with instructions for use, the veterinary practice name and address, and the date.

Midday Phlight having his foreleg bandaged. Giving the horse a haynet helps to reduce fidgeting while you carry out treatment.

Small feeds are often taken more willingly than larger ones, so split the feeds and give them more frequently. This helps to keep up the horse's strength and aids healing, whilst also providing a convenient medium for administering any medicine. On occasions it may be necessary to withhold food. This can be difficult when you are faced with a hungry animal who cannot understand why you won't feed him. But however tempting it may be, do not ignore instructions to withhold food. Always follow your vet's advice.

It is important to make allowances for sick and injured horses and ponies. They are not always rational, and you must of course remain in control for safety's sake, but losing your temper is counterproductive. Be firm but gentle, and take time to coax the patient to do want you want, reassuring them all the time. Once you have a horse's confidence, it is surprising what you can achieve. Bear in mind that the patient may get very stroppy at times, especially when he is starting to recover. In such cases you may have to think fast to protect yourself.

15

2 Be Prepared ────────

Since you can never predict when your horse is likely to be ill or injured, it makes sense to take whatever precautions you can to help you cope in the event of unforeseen problems. In addition to taking practical, day-to-day precautions, which are discussed elsewhere in the book, you must find a good vet, a good farrier, and a good insurance company.

INSURANCE

Insurance is essential, not only to cover your larger veterinary costs in the event of accident or illness , but also to protect you against liability. If your horse or pony causes an accident and you are responsible, the cost of compensating a third party can be vast, quite aside from the veterinary fees that will have to be paid if your animal is injured.

Choose your insurance company with care. They vary a great deal, both in what they are prepared to cover and in the amount you can claim. It is sensible to opt for the company that provides the highest amount of veterinary fees. 'Loss of use' is not easy to claim for. For example, you might buy a competition horse that is not in work and has been off for some time, but on veterinary examination appears unharmed and sound; then, when returning to hard work, the horse promptly breaks down. You may find that in such a circumstance your insurer is unwilling to compensate. Do not automatically assume that if a horse is freeze-branded he must be insured, or insurable. Some horses that are deemed uninsurable are freeze-branded, so unless you know the vendor very well and can trust their word, be cautious when buying a horse that has been off work.

As a general rule, you can have all eventualities insured against, providing you fulfil the regulations. It is extremely important, therefore, that you understand and accept any provisos before committing yourself to one particular policy. Ask the insurance company for clarification of any clauses that you don't understand. Finally, don't buy the first policy you look at; shop around and find the one that will suit your circumstances the best.

Making a Claim

You will increase the chances that your claim will be accepted if you:

- Immediately notify your insurance company of any incident for which you may want to claim. (Always make a note of the time and day you first identified a problem as in most cases this will have to be entered on the claims form.)

- Provide as much detailed information as possible.

- Follow your insurance company's instructions precisely.

IDENTIFICATION

These days it is essential that your horse or pony has some form of permanent identification. Not only is it an effective deterrent to thieves, but a lot of insurance companies give a discount to owners who freeze-brand their horses, or have some other form of identification.

Freeze-brand codes and identichips carry a vast amount of information which is accessible on database. Not only does this help in tracking down stolen animals, but it provides a means of checking that the horse or pony you are buying is indeed the one described. You merely have to contact the firm concerned and they will confirm whether the animal is the correct one.

Freeze-branding

Choose a good company to carry out the branding. Brand numbers are usually preceded by a mark that is unique to the branding company. Each company knows the code mark of its fellow companies.

The area to be branded is clipped closely and cleaned with antiseptic cleaner to guard against infection. Each number and code is then applied, one at a time. The length of time taken to brand a horse depends on the type of breed and coat colour. Thoroughbreds are thin-skinned and require a lighter (shorter) application than say a cob, who has a thicker skin. A grey has to have a stronger brand to ensure that the hair is completely destroyed to

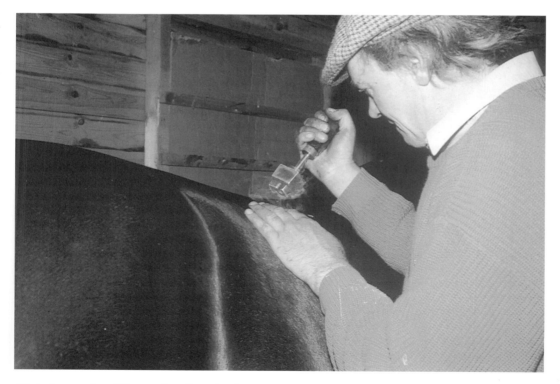

Chris Larcombe of Equestrian Security Services using the branding iron for freeze-marking River Gipsy.

River Gipsy's clear and identifiable freeze-brand mark.

leave a scar because the white hair that normally results from branding is indistinct against the colour of their coat.

Some owners choose to have the brand applied to the shoulder, in front of the saddle, but if branding has been done under the saddle – the usual site – do not ride for about a week. When riding starts, the hair will start to drop off, but do not start riding until any swelling has gone down and the skin has returned to its normal temperature. At this stage, do not pick off the scab or use petroleum jelly or grease on it. It has to establish itself first. Initially the area is very sensitive, and requires a piece of clean sponge or soft sheet under the saddle (cleanliness is very important). Three to four weeks after branding, if any scabs or hair remain, soften them with coconut oil, which comes in solid form in a small jar. Take a small amount and warm it in the palm of your hand, then, using a finger, gently smooth it over the area before brushing it gently to remove the dried skin. Repeat daily, until clear, which takes

a couple of days or so. Do not continue using coconut oil for more than four days: allow a rest period of about six to ten days, and then reapply. This will encourage the white hair to grow clearly.

In addition to the normal freeze-marks, there is a new worldwide copyright combined form from Equestrian Security Services, called the second generation. This can be used on foals from three weeks. It is applied in one go on either side of the neck, under the mane, and takes up much less space than the normal one. It includes country of origin, date of birth and a unique ID number, so it is possible to track horses around the world. It is surprising how far from home horses have been tracked, thanks to this marking.

Identichips

These are microchips containing all the identifying information. They are implanted under the skin by your veterinary surgeon. Never accept anyone who is not qualified or you could risk serious harm and infection. For grey horses, this is a good alternative to the strong branding that they need in order to create a scar (*see above*); and if you have a very valuable horse, then both freeze-branding and an identichip may be worth considering. The chip is inserted in the crest of the horse's neck and, though invisible to the human eye, it is easily detected by a scanner.

Hoof Branding

This is another method of identification. An impression of your postcode is burnt into the wall of the horse's hoof. Your farrier repeats the coding every few months as the hoof horn grows and the code disappears.

THE FARRIER

Choose the best farrier you can find, which is not always easy. Farriers vary a great deal, so ask for recommendations from other horse owners whose judgement you respect.

A good farrier plays a very important role in keeping a horse sound; a bad one can cause untold damage. Not all farriers like the owner watching them at work, but I have always insisted on being present. I will often get on with other work at the same time, but I like to see each foot with the shoe off to check for signs of corns or other trouble lurking under the shoe. If there is a problem under the shoe, the chances are you will not know about it unless you observe shoeing. Some years ago, while at livery and in my absence, River Gipsy had been found to have an

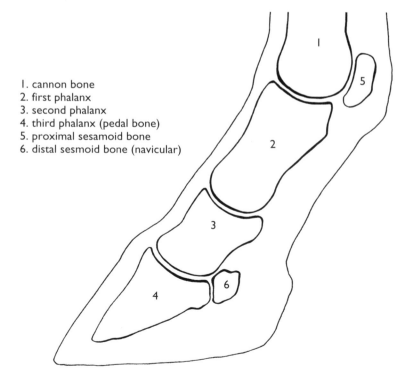

1. cannon bone
2. first phalanx
3. second phalanx
4. third phalanx (pedal bone)
5. proximal sesamoid bone
6. distal sesmoid bone (navicular)

Bones of the lower limb.

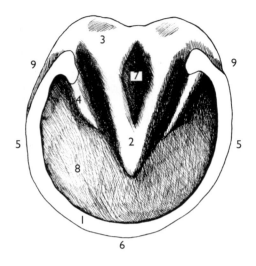

1. hoof wall
2. frog
3. bulb of the heel
4. bar
5. quarters
6. toe
7. cleft of the frog
8. sole
9. heels

The horse's hoof.

abscess under her shoe; the blacksmith had cut it out, and a vet, who had come to look at another horse, had checked it. However, I did not know anything about it until the blacksmith came back a few days later and asked me how she was. Her foot was full of filth and I had quite a bit of work to do on it. Had I been there, I would have known from the start and been able to treat it straight away.

THE VET

If you move to a new district, or acquire a horse or pony for the first time, your first priority must be to find a veterinary practice that is willing and able to care for equine patients. Not all practices do so. Your previous practice might be able to recommend one that has the necessary facilities to provide care to a high standard. This may be especially important if you have competition horses, as the demands of their work may render them more prone to injury. However, accidents can happen under any circumstances, and a well-equipped veterinary practice will make all the difference in emergency cases. If you cannot get personal help in

locating an appropriate practice, you can consult the British Equestrian Directory, which lists registered equine veterinary surgeons in the UK. If you own other animals as well – dogs, cats and so on – it makes sense to choose a practice that has both equine and general animal surgeons.

If you find you really cannot get the results you need from your surgery, or you are at loggerheads with the practice, then it is best to find another. If this becomes necessary, it is advisable to notify the practice in writing. Such matters will need to be dealt with delicately as a new practice may need to contact your previous surgery before taking you on. The British Veterinary Association publishes an excellent leaflet, 'You, Your Animals and Your Veterinary Surgeon: A Guide to Services, Standards and Fees', which every owner should read with care and keep for reference.

Once you have identified the surgery you think will suit you, I would recommend that you make an appointment to meet the surgeon, and then, all being well, register, even if you do not require attention straight away. Along with your name and address it is worth giving the surgery directions to your premises: if you live in a rural district,

Ultrasound scan of the horse's tendons. Dr Sue Dyson at the Animal Health Trust, Newmarket.

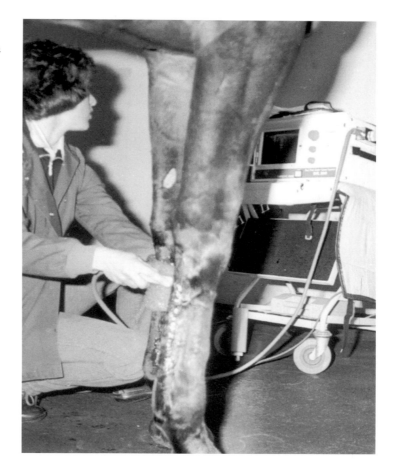

(Below) *A small, portable, X-ray machine, suitable for taking images of the horse's lower joints in his own stable.*

finding the field where you keep your horse can be very difficult. You must also give full written details of all your horses and ponies. This is a wise precaution; the more the vet knows, the faster he can react in an emergency, and speed can be vital. The better a veterinary surgeon knows his patients, the easier it is to diagnose illness, as not all cases are clear from the outset.

You must not be tempted to change from one practice to another and back again repeatedly as fancy takes you. It does not really work. You can always seek a second opinion if you wish it, but do ask your own vet first.

3 Routine Care ————

Good general management plays a vital role in keeping a horse sound, and it is regrettable that many of the ailments that are suffered by horses are entirely preventable. If you establish a daily routine inspection of your horse, there is every chance that you will spot trouble at the start, which can make the difference between a full recovery and lasting damage. Even apparently trivial conditions can become exacerbated by secondary infection. Once you have established your routine, you will find that it is not as time-consuming as you might think.

THE LEGS AND FEET

The legs should be cool and free from swelling. Check them daily with your hands to ensure they have not the slightest heat in them; if they have keep a close eye on them. If the heat and swelling does not reduce, consult your vet. A sound horse will stand comfortably and level, though when relaxed he may rest a hind leg. Shifting the weight repeatedly from one leg to another is a sign of discomfort. A sound horse should trot up evenly with a swinging stride. A

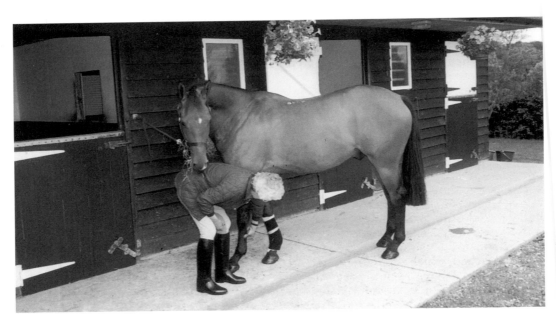

Check the front-limb tendons regularly for signs of strain.

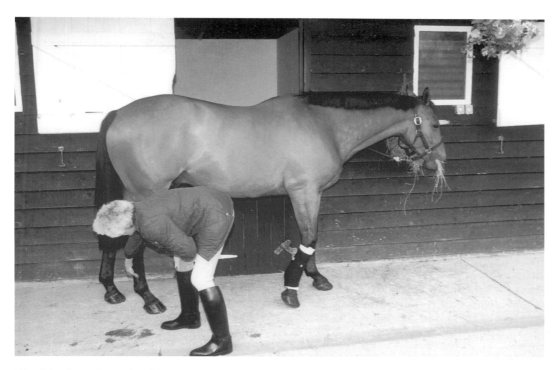

Hind-limb tendons should also be checked for heat or swelling.

happy and healthy horse is a contented horse who enjoys his work.

Sound feet are essential, so do not neglect them. Horses' feet need routine care to prevent problems from ocurring. Whether your horse is shod or unshod, the feet should be picked out every day – morning, evening and after work. This procedure should remove all mud or muck and ensure that there are no stones wedged between the shoe and the frog. Failure to do this properly can result in serious problems, such as bruised soles and infections. I use a hoof-pick with a brush attached, which enables me to clean the feet once I have removed the larger pieces of debris. In addition, I wash the feet to remove any dried-on dirt, and I then disinfect them. A few drops of liquid antiseptic added to warm water is ideal

for this. After washing, leave the feet for a few minutes before feeding them with hoof oil, which should be applied thoroughly with a brush. Use a good-quality, preferably light, oil, which feeds the walls without clogging them.

Shoeing

Shoeing should be carried out every four to six weeks, depending on the amount of work the horse does. The amount of pressure that is exerted on the shoes varies from one horse to another, as does the rate of hoof growth. Excessive growth can cause serious problems, so ensure that the feet are trimmed regularly, regardless of age, and even if the horse is unshod. Trimming the feet of foals and youngsters is as

23

important as it is in older ones – more so in some cases. If the young horse's feet are not kept level, and at the correct length, his limbs will not grow true. With careful trimming from a good farrier, it is surprising how twisted joints can be persuaded to straighten out.

Failure to remove shoes and trim hooves regularly will lead to misalignment of the feet and unnecessary strain, leading to lameness. Cracked hooves can also be caused by overgrown feet. Once they start to crack up, it can take a long time for the cracks to grow out. Cracks must be sealed, and your farrier should deal with them promptly to stop them spreading.

Make sure the feet are trimmed correctly, and that the shoes fit the feet rather than the feet being made to fit the shoes. There should be no sharp edges as these can cause cuts and, in some cases, serious injury through brushing or knocking. Even if you do not require new shoes, the farrier will still remove the shoes and trim the feet. In any case, stick to the four to six weeks rule for really sound feet, however emphatically some people might insist that it can be left longer.

To prevent accidents, ensure the shoes are not loose, or cast off altogether. Cast-offs can be caused by mud, twisting, treading on a piece of metal at the shoe's heel, or by overreaching. If a shoe is loose and coming off, you can – as a very temporary measure – tighten up the clenches: turn down the top piece of nail showing through the hoof wall by using a hammer to tap the head down onto the wall again. If you are out riding when you hear the shoe rattling, a stone may be used in place of the hammer. Call your farrier on your return and do not ride again until the shoe is replaced. If you have to remove the shoe because it is dangerous or painful to leave it on, ensure that you raise all the clenches, as straight as possible, before prising the shoe off with care. A turned-over clench pulled through a hoof wall can cause serious damage, and

may even pull part of the wall away. Check the clenches every day: do not merely look at them; run a finger around the hoof to check that they are flush with the wall. Even new shoes will sometimes rise a few days after shoeing. Risen clenches can cause untold damage, gashing into the other legs, ripping the skin in a jagged way, and this type of injury is often slow to heal.

For normal work, shoes made of steel are required, and these come in various weights. Fast work requires a shoe that is strong, but light enough to prevent strain on the horse's legs. Some shoes have fullering – a groove between the inner and outer edge – and this enables the shoe to grip better, while at the same time weighing less. Most shoes used on riding horses are of this type, though a few are fitted with flat shoes, which weigh a great deal more and can slip. Cart-horses, who are strong and work slowly, often wear flat shoes as the additional weight of the shoe is less significant to them.

The inside edge of a shoe used for riding should be narrowed towards the heel to prevent brushing (when one foot knocks the opposite leg). The shoes are set a tiny distance back from the front of the hind hoof to prevent overreaching (when the hind foot clips the heel of the one in front). Racehorses wear aluminium shoes for extra lightness, but these are not suitable for roadwork. In many cases, injured feet require special surgical shoes, which your farrier will custom make.

The science of shoeing is improving all the time, and nowadays there is a great array of brand-named, 'special shoes' designed to cope with a variety of problems or conditions, so it should be possible to find a suitable one for your horse.

TEETH

It is essential to keep a close check on your horse's teeth, throughout the year and

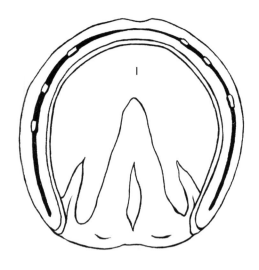

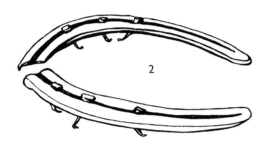

1. A fullered shoe, well seated out. 2. a worn shoe.

regardless of his age. Youngsters are just as likely to need attention as older ones. In young horses, you must make frequent checks to confirm that the permanent teeth are coming through straight and unhindered by the milk teeth. Retained milk teeth will cause the permanent ones to grow out of line, which can ultimately cause serious problems and discomfort. Quick attention can normally save misalignment of the permanent teeth and prevent damage to the inside of the mouth and tongue.

Horses' first (or 'milk') teeth begin to erupt shortly after birth. As the weeks go

First teeth are replaced by permanent teeth as the horse matures. Wolf teeth sometimes have to be surgically removed.

25

by, they teeth arrive two at a time until all are present in front. The first molars (the large teeth at the back of the mouth) come through next, starting with the front molars. As the foal grows and the head becomes bigger, the rest come through. In the horse with a small head, the teeth may be rather restricted for space; and as the permanent teeth replace the milk ones the mouth may become overcrowded. Sometimes it may be necessary to call out your veterinary surgeon to remove any problematic milk teeth, rather than risk their damaging the mouth.

In addition to your own checks, it is essential to have your horse's teeth regularly examined by a qualified professional – either your veterinary surgeon or an equine dentist. Once the teeth become permanent (usually at about four and a half years of age), the professional check should be done every six months; in the younger horse, it is wise to have the teeth checked more often. I remember when River Gipsy was losing her milk teeth that many came out in two pieces and at intervals; when this happens, the retained piece of tooth is often very sharp. Equine dentists may be located in the British Equestrian Directory, or recommended by your vet or a friend. Your horse may be sensitive when having his teeth treated and it is worth trying a variety of experts if you have any concerns over your horse's comfort.

The horse's top jaw is wider than the lower one. This means that the top teeth, which overlap the bottom, will become sharp if they are not rasped regularly. Sharp top teeth will cut the cheeks, and the lower ones will cut the tongue – in either case causing pain and discomfort to the unfortunate victim – so regular rasping is very important. Painful teeth or sore gums and cheeks, can have considerable and far-reaching consequences. To begin with, they will hinder eating; any-

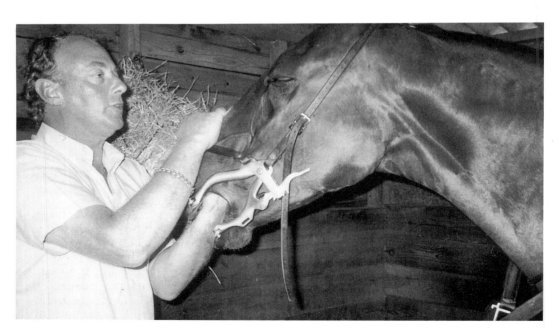

The use of the gag allows a full examination of the horse's mouth.

26

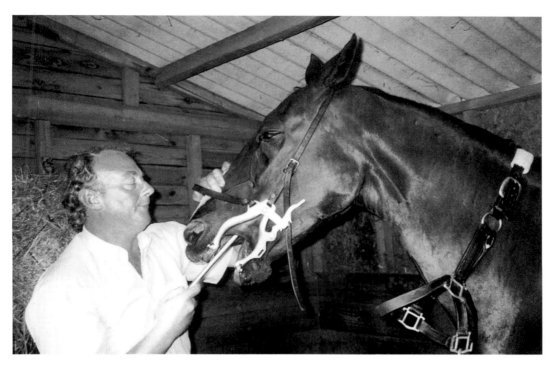

Paul I'anson rasping River Gipsy's teeth with the dental gag in place.

one who has experienced tooth problems will know how painful eating with a toothache can be. If the horse is unable to chew his food properly, digestion may also be inefficient and uncomfortable, which in many cases can lead to weight loss and stomach problems. Furthermore, a painful mouth can make your horse unresponsive or disagreeable when being ridden. These problems will go once the teeth have been treated, although it may take a bit of time to regain the horse's trust that the bit is not going to hurt. Any real damage must be allowed to heal before using a bit; if it is essential that the horse is ridden, a bitless bridle should be used.

Wolf teeth are small rudimentary molars situated in front of the first molar. Not every horse has them. They are similar to wisdom teeth and usually appear when the horse is between five and six years of age. As they interfere with the bit in most cases, and have no real purpose in the mouth, it is wise to have them removed. Normal wolf teeth can be taken out with ease, as their roots are simple, but those that are twisted, or impacted, will require surgery by a vet. In some cases a general anaesthetic may be used. Some teeth can be impacted on the jawbone, just under the surface of the gum, and these can be felt by carefully running a finger over the area.

The suddenness with which these problems can arise is surprising, and in many cases an owner does not suspect that apparent naughtiness or disobedience is actually caused by tooth pain. Both River Gipsy and Castania suffered from wolf-teeth complications in their teens. When

27

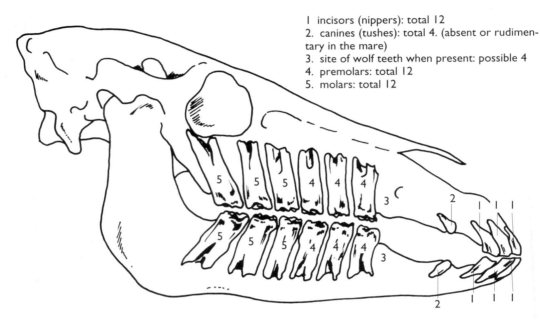

1. incisors (nippers): total 12
2. canines (tushes): total 4. (absent or rudimentary in the mare)
3. site of wolf teeth when present: possible 4
4. premolars: total 12
5. molars: total 12

Dental features of a modern horse.

Castania reared up at a combine one day, I returned to the stable and immediately examined her mouth. I found a loose wolf tooth, tight against the molar. When I took it out, I found that there was an abscess underneath it.

An adult horse has six incisor teeth in the top jaw and six in the lower jaw. Canines are mature teeth that develop in all males and some, but not all, mares. They are single teeth with a point, situated a short space behind the incisors. The molars are big teeth that vary in number, between twelve and fourteen, depending on the amount of wolf teeth (not all come through). Foals have six molars on each jaw to start with. The other three molars come through on each side as permanent teeth, located behind the temporary ones, which is why problems occur when there is a shortage of space. Do check all the teeth are maturing correctly and, if in any doubt, ask advice.

EYES

The eye of a healthy horse should be bright, clear and free from discharge, with the inner lining a pale, salmon-pink colour. Though it is not often mentioned as an essential part of equine husbandry, it is important to check the eyes are regularly; failure to do so can mean neglecting problems that will take a lot of persistence to cure.

Ensure the eyes are kept clean by wiping them daily with a damp piece of cotton wool – using a fresh piece for each eye to prevent infection. Eyes running with thick sludge can cause damage to the skin below the eye, as well as the eye itself. Cleanliness is also especially important in the summer when flies can sting or lay their eggs, in the corner of the eye, as well as spreading infection.

Eyelashes also require regular checking. This may seem trivial but unruly lashes

(Above) *The front teeth and gums, as well as the back teeth, must be checked regularly for plaque deposits or injury.*

River Gipsy with conjunctivitis caused by fly irritation. Conjunctivitis can have serious consequences, and symptoms should always be treated.

Condition

Keep an eye on your horse's general condition. He should be neither too fat nor too thin; the ribs should not show but they should be easily felt when the the skin is gently pressed. A grossly fat horse is as unhealthy as a thin one. Show horses are inclined even now to be too fat, which does them no good. Once fit, their muscles should tone and firm.

You will need to calculate the horse's weight when you worm him (*see* Chapter 4). If you find that your horse has significantly gained or lost weight since the last time you weighed him, you can investigate the possible causes. There may be an underlying problem, but otherwise you can make the necessary adjustments to his diet.

Fat deposits are laid down at 1. the crest 2. over the withers 3. behind the shoulder 4. over the ribs 5. over the quarters and 6. flanks.

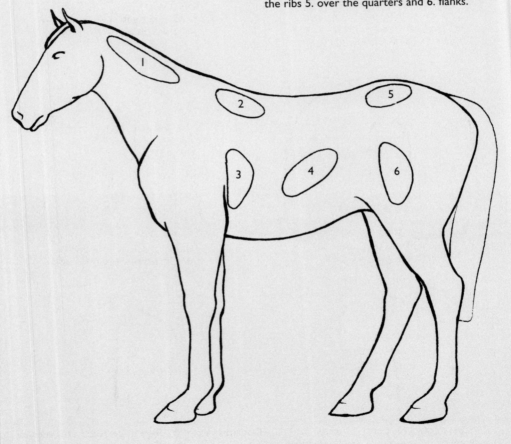

Condition scoring.

Condition

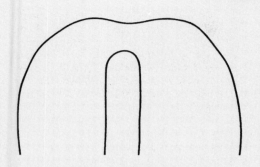

Condition score 5 – obese: very bulging rump; deep gutter along the back; ribs too buried to be felt; marked crest; folds and lumps of fat.

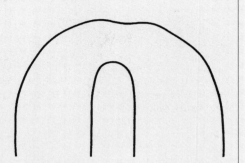

Condition score 4 – fat: rump too well rounded; gutter along the back; ribs and pelvis difficut to feel.

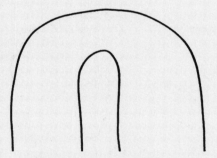

Condition score 3 – good: rump rounded; ribs covered but easy to feel; neck firm; no crest.

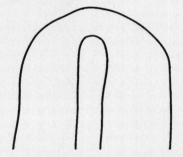

Condition score 2 – thin: rump flat either side of backbone; ribs visible; narrow but firm neck.

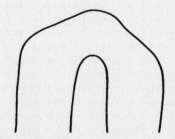

Condition score 1 – poor: rump sunken; cavity under tail; ribs prominent; backbone and croup prominent; ewe neck, narrow and slack.

Condition score 0 – very poor: rump very sunken; deep cavity under tail; skin tight over prominent bones; backbone and pelvis very prominent; marked ewe neck, very narrow.

Condition scoring. The horse should be neither too fat nor too thin. Here, River Gipsy is recovering from an injury inflicted by wire, spring 1992.

will cause irritation and may scratch the surface of the eye, leading to partial blindness. To check, stand in front of the horse's head and examine the way the lashes and brows are growing. In general eyelashes grow outwards and curl slightly upwards, but in reality the odd one will invert, and these are the ones to check for. If found, use a pair of sterilized blunt-ended scissors to very carefully snip off the offending lash. If in doubt, call your veterinary surgeon straight away. Time counts. Also check for bits of hay, grass, grit, or any foreign bodies, for these can cause serious damage too.

COAT

Regardless of breed, the coat should have a healthy gloss, and the skin should be supple. When the horse is in action, the skin should move fluidly over the muscle. A test for elasticity is to pinch the skin on the neck and then release it. Healthy skin will spring back to normal straight away.

Tight, dry, bald or scabby skin is unhealthy and will need attention. While at grass, although ungroomed, the summer coat should still shine. The ungroomed coat has a soft layer of grease to protect it against bad weather, naturally this will grow thicker with the coat in the winter; the greater the degree of grease, the better the protection. Although the winter coat is not as glossy as it is in summer, it should still maintain a degree of shine in its dry state. Brushing with a body brush will remove the grease from the coat so care should be taken when grooming horses at grass. When out at grass, the tips of the coat may rise, as opposed to their flat position when the horse is stabled or warm.

4 Worming and Vaccination ─────────

A preoccupation with saving time and money is false economy. A little forethought and some judiciously spent money can prevent many illnesses, diseases, and even certain accidents, all of which can prove remarkably costly, not just in veterinary fees but also in loss of the use of your horse.

The prevention of illness is a matter of common sense. However, too often, far too great an amount of faith is placed in the idea that things are more likely to go well than badly, and that there is no need to take precautions. How often one hears irresponsible owners accusing others of being 'paranoid' because they are taking the trouble to be sensible and caring. In this chapter, I shall look at some of the simple ways you can protect your horse from unnecessary illness.

WORMING

This heads the list of sensible preventative measures. Even nowadays, one hears of owners proudly boasting that they have not used wormers for several years, believing that their horses will be immune to any problems if they are kept in a large field. It is true that a worm explosion is less likely in a large field supporting only a few horses than it is in more crowded conditions where horses and ponies graze continuously and the droppings are not removed on a regular basis. Overcrowding and/or poor

pasture management place the animals in grave danger of suffering a massive worm burden. Keeping your paddock clean will help to cut down the risk of contamination from infective larvae – the stage of the worm's lifecycle when it is passed out with droppings and picked up by horses from grass while grazing. Nevertheless, however good your pasture management, you must worm regularly, according to the manufacturer's instructions and your veterinary surgeon's advice. At intervals ask your vet to carry out a test on the fresh droppings to ensure that the wormers are working and that there is no build-up (which can happen when resistance occurs to some brands of wormer).

Types of parasite

Different worms have different lifecycles, and an understanding of this is important in their effective treatment and prevention.

Worms that require controlling come in two groups, adult and immature:

Adult group

Large strongyles
(large redworm): *Strongylus vulgaris*
Strongylus edentatus
Strongylus equinus
Triodontophorus
species

Small strongyles
(small redworms): *Cyathostome* species

Pinworms: *Oxyuris equi*
Ascarids (large
roundworm): *Parascaris equorum*

Lungworms: *Dictyocaulus arnfieldi*

Intestinal
threadworms: *Strongyloides westeri*

Large mouth/
stomach worms: *Habronema muscae*

Stomach
hairworms: *Trichostrongylus axei*

Immature group

Lungworms: *Dictyocaulus arnfieldi*

Large Strongyles
(large redworms): *Strongylus vulgaris*
(arterial stages)
Strongylus edentatus
(tissue stages)

Small strongyles
(small redworms): *Cyathostome* species

Pin worms: *Oxyuris equi*

Ascarids (large
roundworms): *Parascaris equorum*

Neck
threadworms: *Onchocera* species
(Microfilariae)

In addition to the above, there are two other important parasites:

Bots: *Gastrophilus* species
(oral and gastric)

Tapeworms: *Anoplocephala perfoliata*

Types of Wormer

There are three main types of wormer, each containing distinct chemicals:

1. The macrocyclic lactones.

These are made up of the avermectins and milbemycins.

Ivermectin is an avermectin, which is used in Eqvalan and Furexel brands.

The milbemycins are a new class of drug containing moxidectin, which is used in Equest.

Bots

Bots are in fact flies belonging to the *Oestridae* family (of which warble flies are also a member), and their maggot forms are parasitic. They lay yellow eggs on the horse's coat, mainly visible on the legs and shoulders. The irritation they cause incites the horse to lick them off, and they are then swallowed to continue their life cycle internally. If they hatch before being swallowed, they burrow their way through the skin, and thence to the intestine. Ivermectin (such as Eqvalan) used in the autumn will control them; otherwise they can cause a lot of damage. Remove the yellow eggs as soon as you spot them. They can usually be scraped off, but if they are very numerous, you may need to resort to clipping. Dispose of the eggs carefully to ensure they are not picked up again. Fly repellents will help to keep bots away, but be aware that some repellents contain Tolvene, which is a banned substance in competition. Thus, if you are competing you horse or pony, be sure to read the labels on your repellents and avoid those containing Tolvene. In the past, bot eggs were a common sight on horses and ponies at grass; although there seems to be less occurrences in recent years, bots are still a great plague to horses and other animals.

---

2. The pyrimidines.
These include Pyrantel, which is used in Strongid P.

3. The benzimidazoles.
These are a family of four different chemicals. The first is Fenbendazole (used in Panacur), the second is Mebendazole (used in Telmin and Equivurm Plus), and the third and fourth are Febantel and Oxibendazole which are used in other brands.

From this it will be understood that when you change the brand you do not necessarily change the drug. It is imperative therefore to read the instructions.

Different chemical families control a varied number of the parasites. Ivermectin and moxidectin will control all the above-mentioned parasites except tapeworm. (To protect against tapeworm, a double the standard dose of pyrantel is required.)

Pyrantel controls the large and small strongyles (redworms), pinworms, and

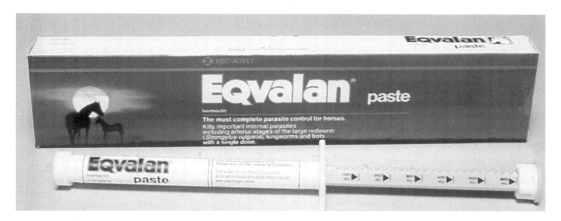

For the treatment and control of lungworm, bots and immature redworm larvae, ivermectin and moxidectin are widely available.

(Below) *A double dose of the substance Pyrantel is still the only effective way of eliminating tapeworm from the horse.*

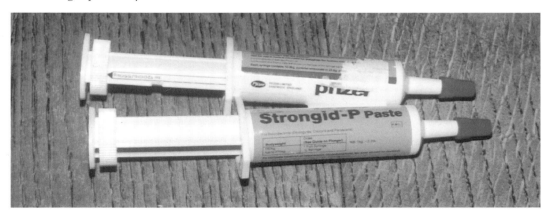

ascarids (large roundworms), during their adult stage.

Fenbendazole will cope with the adult stage of the large strongyles (large redworms), pinworms (adult and immature stages), and ascarids (large roundworms).

Small redworms do not always respond these days. Intestinal threadworms (adult) require seven times the standard dose, while the immature stage of the large strongyle (large redworm) needs the standard dose on five consecutive days. The immature stage of the small redworm requires the standard dose for five consecutive days or a single treatment at four times the dose. One standard dose of ivermectin (Eqvalan) seems to me a far more sensible choice. I use Eqvalan, and then give Strongid P for tapeworms.

As a rule, wormers are expensive, but some mail-order firms can supply most brands a comparatively cheaply. An added advantage of buying wormers in this way is that they arrive fresh, as you would expect from a veterinary practice, while some shops will sell stock right up to the use-by date. If you order wormers by mail in the UK, you will have to enclose written confirmation that you are the owner or keeper of equines and that you will not be reselling any wormers sent to you. This is a requirement laid down by the Royal Pharmaceutical Society, with whom mail-order firms have to be registered. Wormers are also obtainable from some chemists and saddlers, as well as feed merchants (if registered), and your veterinary practice.

Using Wormers

Follow the manufacturer's recommendations with regard to the length of time that should elapse between using each wormer. The required length of time varies according to the group they are linked to. The frequency with which one type of wormer is administered varies not only from one brand to another but from one time of year to another. And foals will usually require a different dose and/or frequency of worming. So it bears repeating that you should always read the instructions for each wormer whenever you use it, and not simply rely on your memory of what you did the last time.

It is up to individual preference which form of wormer is used. Paste-form wormers must be administered with a plastic syringe, which may be expensive. However, they do at least allow you to be sure that the recipient has received the correct dose. Granules are the other popularly used form of wormer, and these are intended to be mixed with feed rather than given directly. The only problem that may occur is that your horse may affect

---

Using a Syringe

Take the syringe in your right hand, if you are right-handed, and stand on the off side of your horse. (If you are left-handed place the syringe in your left hand, and stand on the near side). Take the headcollar with the spare hand to hold the head steady. Then, with care and precision, insert the nozzle of the syringe into the corner of the mouth, entering at the place where the bit lies, and press the handle carefully to release the paste onto the tongue. Some wormers, such as Eqvalan, contain a full dose in a small quantity, so one can, in most cases, administer it in one go. Other types require larger quantities to constitute a full dose, which means that you may have to give the dose in smaller amounts to enable the recipients to swallow the paste. Be careful that the horse does not spit it out: hold the head up for a few seconds until he has swallowed.

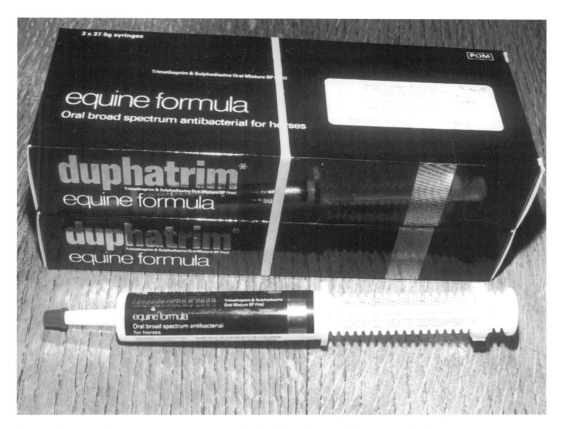

The oral syringe is a convenient means of administering medication to the horse.

Quarantine

To prevent any risk of infecting your current stock, worm newcomers with a good compound wormer such as Eqvalan, and then keep them stabled for forty-eight hours. You do not know at that stage if they are able to take a brand, Benzimidazoles based. When moving from one field to another, worm all the occupants twenty-four hours beforehand to ensure that the pasture is kept as worm-free as possible. All field or stable occupants should be wormed on the same day. If this is done, and the droppings are removed regularly, the worms should be under control.

---

the palatability of the feed and your horse may refuse to eat it.

As time has a habit of passing rather fast, it is wise to replace a wormer as soon as you have used it, then you can keep your worming calendar accurate. Wormers should be stored in a safe, cool place, away from children and other animals. Horse wormers are intended for equine use only, not for cats or dogs. Do not smoke or eat while handling wormers, and always wash you hands after use. I would also recommend that as an added precaution you wear disposable gloves.

Calculating the dose

In order to worm your horse or pony correctly it is essential to know his correct weight. A weighbridge will give you the best results, if you have access to one. However, they are not easily available to ordinary owners, so one has to rely on more traditional methods. Some calculate the weight from girth measurement and reference chart, but this is not as accurate as the following formula:

$$\text{Weight (kg)} = \frac{\text{girth (cm}^2) \times \text{length (cm)}}{11,900}$$

(length = point of shoulder to point of buttocks [*tuber ischii*])

In order to calculate your horse's length you will need a long, flexible tape measure, the type you can rewind into a case is best. Measuring can be done in a variety of ways; shoulder to buttock (In my experi-ence I have found this to be the most accurate); over the shoulder to tail; and over the elbow to buttock. I once rode River Gipsy onto a farm weighbridge and then compared the results with those calculated with the above formula. Having deducted my weight and that of the tack, plus the few pounds the weighbridge operator told me to, the results were the same.

VACCINATION

Vaccination is essential, not only for your own horse's safety, but for other people's animals. Horses and ponies that compete in any sphere must be vaccinated before they are allowed to enter, as must brood-mares before going to stud. This does not mean that other owners need not vacci-nate their horses if they are only used for hacking, or kept in fields on their own. The flu virus can be passed from one horse to another very easily. An infected horse

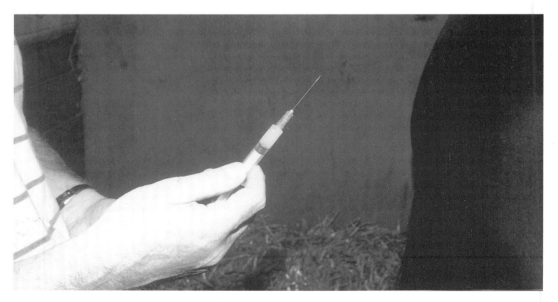

Yearly vaccinations are an essential part of the horse's protection against diseases like tetanus and influenza.

can pass the virus to another, over quite long distances merely by coughing when the wind is in another horse's direction.

There are now three diseases that require vaccinating against.

Equine Influenza

Equine influenza vaccination requires a primary course, then boosters. The primary two-dose course usually starts with foals at five months of age, while adults can receive their first injection at any time providing they are healthy and free from disease. The second part of the course follows some weeks later, depending on the brand of vaccination. Thereafter, boosters are given at set intervals, the length of which depends once again on the brand used. Some foals may have an increased susceptibility to influenza if their intake of colostrum is inadequate, in which case they may need an early single injection at two to three months of age, followed by the two-dose primary course at five months of age. Your veterinary surgeon will know the exact timing of the primary and booster doses. Choose a brand that provides the most advanced protection, as the influenza virus strains keep changing. The annual booster should not exceed the anniversary date, for even a day late is unacceptable for regulatory authorities, such as the Jockey Club. A missed booster means starting from scratch again, as if the horse had never been vaccinated, a long and costly mistake. In some circumstances – when there are a lot of influenza cases in the area, for example – it is wise to have the booster earlier. Consult your vet to decide if it is necessary.

Equine Herpes Virus (EHV)

Equine Herpes Virus (EHV) is another virus against which it is very wise to vaccinate. It is the third on the list of annual or biannual routine vaccinations horses and ponies require for protection. It is now widely recognized as a major cause of infectious respiratory disease, in addition to causing mares to abort their foals in some cases. The virus has also been shown to be immune suppressive, which means that an infected horse is more susceptible to other viruses or bacteria. There are two forms – EHV 1 and EHV 4 – both of which are present within the horse population. Solvay Duphar have developed a vaccine to control both, for a recent survey has shown that over 80 per cent of the horse population could already be carrying a latent EHV. For this reason it is wise for owners to consider adding this vaccination to the previous two. Respiratory problems need controlling and every one you can control is one less they are likely to suffer from. Like the influenza vaccination course, EHV requires a two-dose primary course starting at five months of age. Should there be an increased risk of early exposure to field infection with EHV 1 or EHV 4, or a foal has consumed insufficient colostrum, the foal should receive a single dose at three months of age, followed by the full primary vaccination course at five months. Thereafter, horses and ponies should usually receive a booster every six months. Incidentally, like other vaccinations, only healthy horses and ponies can start the course.

Tetanus

Tetanus is another important disease that horses must be protected from. Some areas of the UK are far more prone to tetanus occurrence than others, but you should never take any risks; always ensure your horse is vaccinated. A tiny scratch or puncture wound that hardly shows can allow entry to the organism that causes the disease. So ensure your horse or pony is

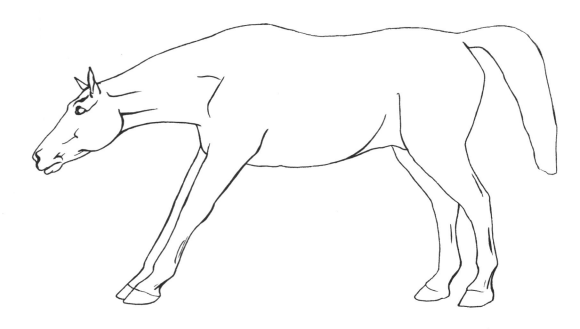

Tetanus.

protected as soon as is practical and preferably from twelve weeks of age. Foals sometimes have to have an injection against tetanus at birth if they are deemed to be particularly at risk. The tetanus vaccination normally consists of two injections, four to six weeks apart, with a booster every two years, thereafter. Once the initial course is finished, the equine influenza and tetanus boosters can in many cases be given as one single injection, alternating each year with the equine influenza vaccine on its own. The vaccination information is entered on a vaccination certificate, dated and signed by the veterinary surgeon.

Tips for Vaccination

- As injections need to be given into a deep muscle, I always have my horses injected in their hindquarters. If the neck is used then the only suitable area is just in front of the shoulder, where it joins the neck.

- There is no need to stop exercising after an injection, but take it gently for forty-eight hours. I like to give the vaccination on the horse's day off, and then give him quiet exercise the following day, before resuming ordinary work,

- If you opt for the combined equine influenza and tetanus vaccine, make sure that the horse's vaccination record is checked each year to avoid the possibility of your horse being accidentally vaccinated for the same disease two years running.

5 Know your Horse: Signs & Symptoms

First and foremost, it is important for every horse owner or carer to know the meaning of the term 'soundness', and how it applies to the horse's day-to-day maintenance. A basic understanding will enable a watchful minder to know when the horse is unwell, and to determine when the horse needs specialist care.

It is essential to check every day that your horse or pony is fit and well. Specific symptoms of various illnesses differ, but there are some signs that are common to most in that they indicate that something is not right. When going down to the stables in the morning, note how the horse reacts. Is he bright and alert, ready for his food? Or is he dull and uninterested? Has he eaten up the food from the night before? When you know your horse, you will be familiar with his normal habits and be able to recognize any behaviour that is out of character. For example, some horses may be fussy and habitually leave some of their food; others will never leave anything. Whichever is the case, you should investigate if your horse suddenly starts behaving differently from normal.

Check how much water has been drunk since the bucket was last filled last thing the night before. Fresh, clean water is vital to keep a horse healthy and should be available at all times, in the stable and at grass. The quantity consumed is a key pointer to some problems, although amounts may vary according to the weather. A lack of water can cause dehydration and with it illness.

How is the horse standing? Is he standing alert and inquisitive, or is he dull with his head down, looking dejected? If the latter, then he may be unwell and need a close examination. When he moves around the box, is he moving easily or is he dragging a leg? Or is he having difficulty standing four square on his feet? Is his nose

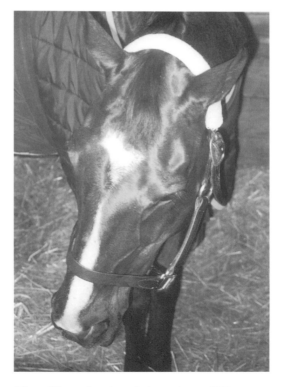

River Gipsy showing obvious signs of illness: (see page 121) always call the vet immediately.

41

1. skull
2. mandible
3. atlas
4. axis
5. cervical vertebrae
6. thoracic vertebrae
7. lumbar vertebrae
8. sacrum
9. cocygeal vertebrae
10. pelvis

11. scapula
12. humerus
13. radius (and ulna)
14. ribs
15. femur
16. tibia (and fibula)
17. carpal bones
18. cannon bone
19. tarsal bones
20. first phalanx
    (long pastern bone)
21. second phalanx
    (short pastern bone)
22. third phalanx (pedal bone)

23. sternum
    a. first rib
    b. Olecranon
    c. accesssory carpal bone
    d. proximal sesamoid bones
    e. distal sesamoid
       (navicular) bone
    f. patela
    g. tuber calcani
    h. splint bone
    i. tuber coxae
    j. greater trochanter
    k. ischium

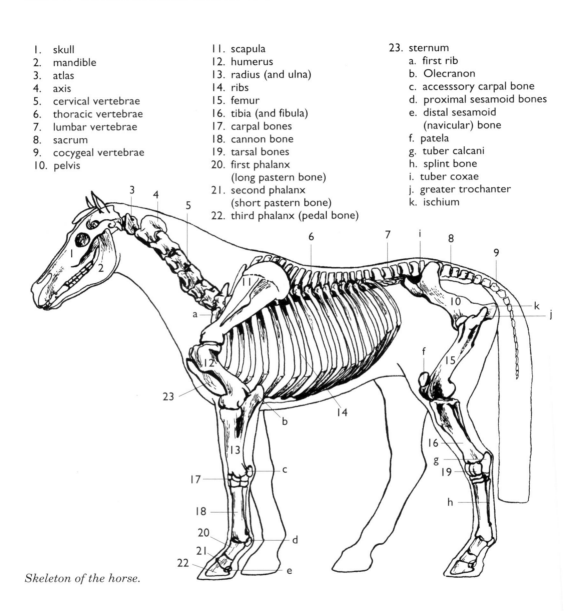

Skeleton of the horse.

clean, with no sign of a cough or a wheeze? Is the inside of the eye the correct pale, salmon-pink colour?

These are just some of the points to note when checking your horse in the stable or in the field. Such routine checks should become habitual; and if there is anything that you are not quite sure about you must seek advice. Never ignore unexplained symptoms, however trivial they may seem: quick action is so often the key to preventing more serious illness.

a. levator nasolabialis
b. lateral nostril dilator
c. masseter
d. zygomaticus
e. parotidoauricularis
f. orbicularis oculi
g. brachiocephalicus
h. splenius
i. rhomboideus
k. sternocephalicus
l. trapezius

m. subclavius
n. supraspinatus
o. deltoideus
p. triceps
q. latissimus dorsi
r. extensor carpi radialis
s. common digital extensor
t. extensor carpi ulnaris
u. lateral digital extensor
v. flexor carpi radialis
w. flexor carpi ulnaris
x. pectoralis
y. serratus ventralis thoracis
z. external abdominal oblique

aa. tensor fasciae latae
bb. superficial gluteal
cc. biceps femoris
dd. semitendinosus
ee. long digital extensor
ff. lateral digital extensor
ii. deep digital flexor
ll. popliteus
mm. tibialis caudalis
nn. gastrocnemius

1. common extensor tendon
2. lateral extensor tendon
3. interosseus medius
   (suspensory apparatus)
4. deep digital flexor tendon
5. superficial flexor tendon

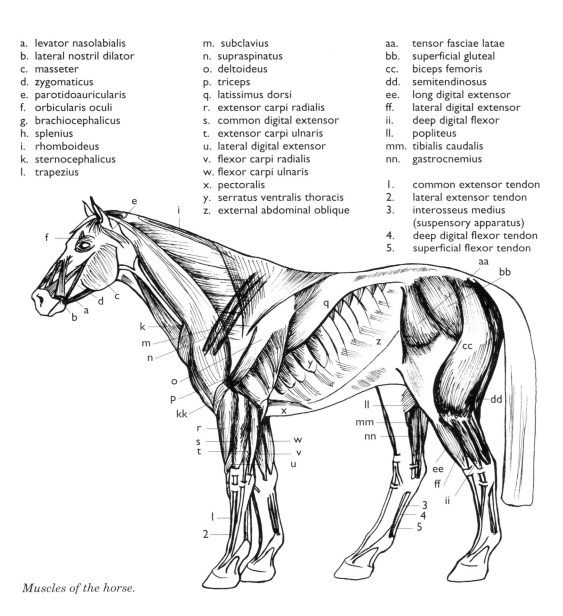

Muscles of the horse.

TEMPERATURE

As with humans, the horse's temperature, is a very good indicator of his state of health. As a general rule, the horse's nor-mal temperature is 100.5°F (38°C), with a variance of 0.5°F (−17.5°C). Since it varies slightly from one horse to another, it is worth finding out what your own horse's normal temperature is so that you can more accurately judge when he is feeling off colour.

One degree over is not normally serious, but two degrees can be, and anything above that is very serious indeed. When River Gipsy's temperature soared to over 103.6°F (39.7°C) compared to her normal reading of 100°F (37.7°C) or just under, her surgeon knew just how ill she was. I was able to monitor her temperature and keep the vet informed of any changes. Had I not had a thermometer, this would have been impossible.

PULSE

The pulse rate varies according to the horse's general health, but it is also affected by other factors. The age of the horse is one – the very old and the very young have a faster rate – as is climate. Sleep or

---

Taking a Horse's Temperature

YOU WILL NEED:

- A veterinary thermometer.
- Petroleum jelly.
- A watch with a second hand.
- Notebook and pen.

Before you start you must be sure that the thermometer is scrupulously clean. Do not be tempted to use an ordinary thermometer; buy the veterinary sort, which has a strong cap on the top to allow you to hold it firmly, and also to prevent its being sucked into the rectum.

1. Shake the thermometer to ensure that it is reading well below normal, and then smear it with petroleum jelly to ease its insertion.

2. Stand alongside the horse's hip, and gently but firmly take hold of the dock of the tail. Some people push the tail up with the left hand, but I find it upsets the horse less if you pull it towards you.

3. Carefully insert the thermometer, gently easing into the horse's rectum, and hold it there securely for just over a minute. Correct timing is very important, so watch the second hand, rather than the minute hand, to ensure that you obtain a true temperature.

4. Loosen your grip on the tail very slightly (but do not let go); this will relax the horse and ensure that the anus is tight around the thermometer.

5. After one minute, extract the thermometer, wipe off the petroleum jelly, and read the result.

Each time you take your horse's temperature, make a note of the result, together with the date and time, so that you can build a regular record of your horse's temperature in sickness and in health.

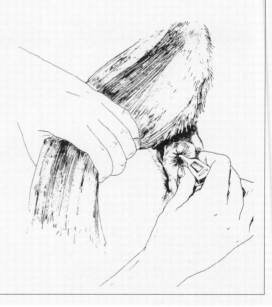

Taking the temperature correctly with a digital thermometer.

Taking a Horse's Pulse

There are two arteries that come near accessible surfaces and can therefore be used to gauge a horse's pulse rate: one passes over the lower jawbone, just below the point where the windpipe joins the throat, under the cheekbone; the other is located at the top of the forearm in line with the elbow.

YOU WILL NEED:

- A watch with a second hand.
- Notebook and pen.

1. Place your fingers gently on top of the artery, applying pressure until you can feel the pulse.

2. Count the beats over a period of one minute, using the seconds-hand of your watch to keep time. When you have an accurate reading, write it down for record.

The author taking Midday Phlight's pulse.

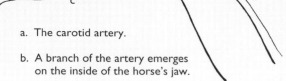

a. The carotid artery.

b. A branch of the artery emerges on the inside of the horse's jaw.

c. The pulse can be felt where the artery lies directly on the jaw bone and curves towards the outside of the face.

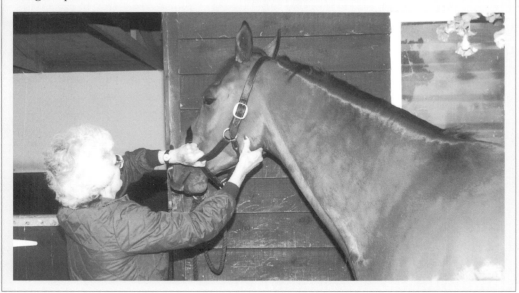

unconsciousness will slow the rate, while exercise will increase it. In fit, healthy horses the rate should rapidly return to normal when the activity ceases. (This is why competition horses are checked during work at various stopping points: if the pulse rate does not return to normal within a given time, the horse may have to retire from the event.) Fevers induce a higher pulse rate, and the higher it is the worse the fever. A pulse rate that is slower or weaker than is normal for the individual horse and his level or activity may indicate a non-febrile disease (diseases not related to fevers). The horse's normal pulse at rest is 36–42 beats per minute.

RESPIRATION

Respiration, like the pulse-rate, varies according to the horse's activities, age and work. At rest the normal adult rate is eight to twelve breaths per minute. The breathing rate is slower when the horse is resting, sleeping or unconscious. The larger the horse, the slower the rate. For example, a Shetland pony may have a reading of twelve beats per minute, compared to a Shire horse's reading of only eight. A youngster will breathe faster than an adult, while

---

Taking a Horse's Breathing Rate

A veterinary surgeon can determine the breathing rate by using a stethoscope to listen to the heart and lungs. Owners can assess it less scientifically by watching the flank going in and out, which should be smooth and without effort. Using a watch with a second hand, watch the breathing and count for a minute. Another method involves placing a hand gently on the flank, firm enough to feel the breathing motions. However a stethoscope is essential for a true reading, so if in any doubt concerning your horse's breathing rate, contact your vet.

---

mares (especially when pregnant) have a faster rate then males. If the rate is above normal when tested at rest, there could be something wrong. For example, the respiration rate will rise with a fever, and veterinary advice may be required. In addition to exercise, emotional states such as stress, fear and excitement, will all push the breathing rate up. Once the horse is calm or at rest, it should return to the normal rate.

Even if your horse is fit, it is wise to have the heart and lungs checked annually. This is especially important if the horse is in his teens, and it can easily be arranged to coincide with a vaccination renewal. Regular checks will also reassure your insurance company that your horse's health is monitored. Thus, should a problem arise, you can confirm to your insurance company that your horse was fit when insured. This can make a vast difference should you need to claim.

FAECES

The colour of the faeces varies according to the type of food the horse is eating. Grass will make the droppings green. Their consistency will vary according to the condition of the grass from moist to normal; but they should not be loose. Loose droppings that are similar to cowpats and smell unusual should be regarded with suspicion, as they could signify problems in the intestine. If this condition rights itself within a short time, the horse or pony probably just ate something that did not quite agree. On the other hand if it persists or becomes worse, call in veterinary help in case it is serious.

A healthy horse, stabled and on a suitable corn, or corn-based diet, plus hay, should have golden brown droppings that are firm, but crack on contact with the ground, having passed out easily without effort. If on a low protein diet, such as mixed nuts or mixed concentrates, the droppings

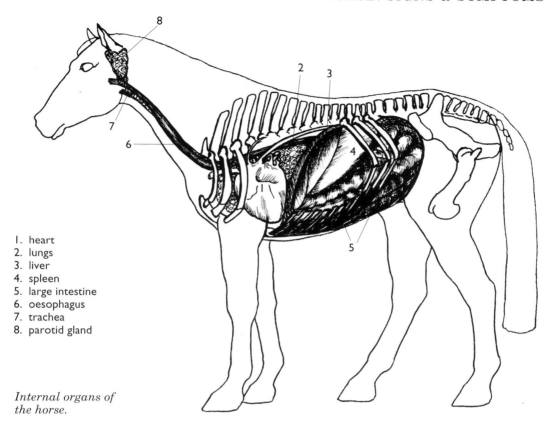

1. heart
2. lungs
3. liver
4. spleen
5. large intestine
6. oesophagus
7. trachea
8. parotid gland

Internal organs of the horse.

may contain a substantial amount of dried grass. This may affect the colour of the droppings, turning them a darker shade.

Constipation is often indicated by small droppings that are dry and hard. This will occur if your horse is not fed the correct amount of roughage. It causes discomfort and should be dealt with swiftly before other complications arise.

Droppings should be passed about eight times every twenty-four hours. This will depend on the content and amount of the food. Three to four more secretions is not always unusual, but less than eight could indicate a problem.

When fit, the approximate size of droppings for a 15.2hh. horse is two inches by three inches. This will vary according to the size of the horse or pony. Make a note of the size your horse normally passes, so that should it alter by a marked amount you will be aware that something may be wrong. The droppings from a fit horse should not smell unpleasant, providing the stable is perfectly clean. There is no need for an unpleasant smell, either on horse or your own clothes. However, seasonal changes may affect the potency of such smells, for example, in the summer; and when a mare is in season, droppings often smell worse.

URINE

Staling, as passing urine is referred to in the equine world, happens several times a

47

day, depending on the amount of water consumed and the weather condition.

The colour and consistency of the urine in a healthy horse varies, both in the stable and at grass, from pale yellow (basically clear) to a much darker and thicker substance. If it is very dark this could be related to a health problem and your vet should be consulted. If a horse is ill, a urine sample is often tested to see if it can give any helpful information, as it is excretion produced by the kidneys, and helps to maintain the body's water balance. The odour is characteristic and at times has varying degrees of ammonia. When a mare is in season the ammonia smell is stronger and, after staling, the floor may be marked and sticky, as if with egg-white.

The stable floor should be swept daily and disinfected on a regular basis to pro-

mote cleanliness. Wet bedding should be picked out in the evenings, in addition to keeping the horse's rug as clean and dry possible, to reduce the risk of infection. Horse's can be encouraged to stale by shaking straw or whistling and will prefer to do so on soft ground, such as grass or their own bedding. The urine of herbivorous animals that eat grass is usually alkaline; but those that eat oats and hay as well as grass, as in the case of horses, may produce an acid urine. This is another reason behind the importance of dry bedding, to protect from the acid urine.

BLOOD TESTS

Not all illnesses are caused by diseases or viruses. Secondary infection and poisoning be responsible for just as many problems. Since there are any number of possible causes – not the least of which is neglected wounds that then become infected – your veterinary surgeon may have to take a blood sample to determine a specific agent.

A special syringe is used to draw the blood out of the artery in the side of the neck, near the windpipe (the artery and windpipe run side by side). Only a veterinary surgeon can do this as knowledge and sterile equipment are essential. In some cases, the test results can be obtained at the surgery; in others, which are perhaps more complicated, may necessitate sending the sample to go to a laboratory. It can take a day or two to come through. The test results will enable the vet to determine what has to be treated and enable the surgeon to administer the appropriate drugs.

Blood tests may also be taken from fit horses to check that there is no trouble brewing. Competition horses are the ones normally tested to ensure all is well. They are being worked hard and need a high-performance feeds, which can cause problems. Testing can prevent trouble.

Dark-green, foul-smelling sludge in place of the normal dung, indicating a severe gastrointestinal disturbance (see Chapter 10).

6 The Veterinary Cupboard

The first-aid kit and other related items that make up what I call the veterinary cupboard are essential in any stable yard, regardless of size. The only difference between a yard housing just a few horses and one of dozens should be the quantity of items.

Ensure that the cupboard is well out of reach from children and inquisitive animals. All drugs must be kept under security, as with human medication; it is your responsibility, so do not take risks. Return any medications that have passed their expiry date to your veterinary practice and, if necessary, request replacements. Keep the equipment clean and updated, replacing any items that have been used up. Not long ago a young girl in our village knocked on my door, the owner of a horse where she helped out in order to ride herself, had had an accident, cutting the horse quite badly. The veterinary surgeon that came out wished for the legs to be bandaged and dressed after she had left. The veterinary cupboard was empty. Mercifully, I had enough bandages and gamgee, and once applied all was well.

What you choose to keep can vary, but there are a number of essential items that

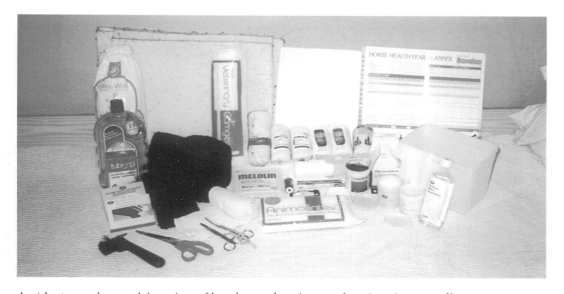

Accidents can happen! A variety of bandages, dressings and antiseptics, as well as scissors, are essential for prompt first aid.

should form the basis of any veterinary cupboard. Not all of these items have to be purchased through your veterinary practice. Supplies of basics such as cotton wool, surgical spirit, disposable gloves, and so on, can be obtained off the shelf in either a chemist, a saddler, or, in many cases, a feed merchant.

DRESSINGS AND BANDAGES

Poultice

A poultice is a padded dressing that draws out pus and/or foreign bodies from wounds, abscesses, and other injuries.

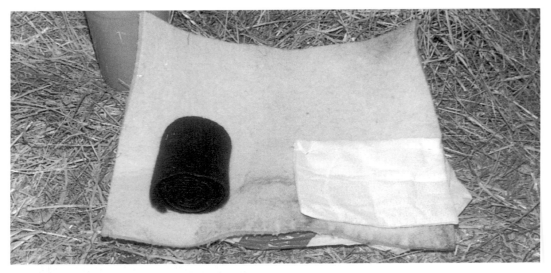

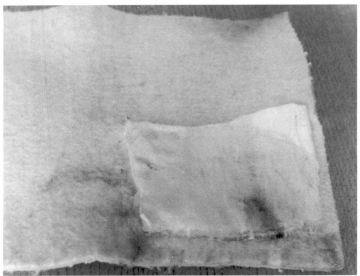

(Above) *Applying a poultice to any wound helps to prevent the infection from spreading to the surrounding tissue.*

When changing the poultice, look for signs of discharge.

Applying Animalintex Poultice

YOU WILL NEED:

- Animalintex
- A pan of hot, boiled water
- A pad of gamgee or fibregee
- A surgical or stable bandage
- Two plates (optional)
- Needle and thread (optional)

1. Cut Animalintex to the required size.

2. Soak in the hot, boiled water.

3. When heated, remove from the water and squeeze out. I find squeezing out between two clean plates the easiest method.

4. Allow to cool to blood temperature, and then apply.

5. Apply the gamgee or fibregee pad

6. Secure with the bandage.

It can be quite difficult sometimes to keep the poultice from slipping off the wound; to solve this problem I have taken to stitching the four corners of the poultice to the gamgee pad before soaking it, which means that there is only the one dressing to apply before bandaging.

There are other advantages. If the horse starts to fidget or get stroppy, you have a better chance of keeping it clean and safe in your hand – dropping poultices is expensive! The dressing stays where it should until removed for replacement, even in tricky places on the fetlock. You can turn them out too, or exercise if necessary and all right to do so. It takes longer to apply but is worth it.

Never apply a poultice directly over a joint, and be sure to renew the poultice every twelve hours.

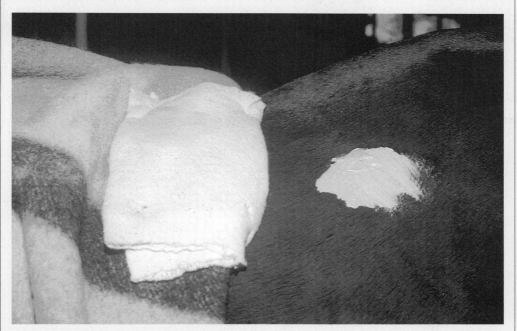

A kaolin poultice applied to the shoulder, in this case to draw out shotgun pellets from River Gipsy. The poultice was secured by stitching the dressing into the blanket.

Poultices are also useful for sprains, bruising, skin disorders such as mud fever, and foot problems such as corns and laminitis. Animalintex is a popularly used padding and gauze, poultice dressing which can be used in the conventional manner as well as bandaged on to the leg in a dry state to relieve or prevent swelling after work.

Gamgee

This is a sterile pad made of cotton wool covered with absorbent gauze. This comes in rolls of two widths – twelve inches (30cm) and eighteen inches (45cm). It is used to either support or protect the legs and keep the tendons and muscles warm. In addition it also prevents bandages from marking the legs, which can cause damage, in the stables, at work or exercise and travelling. Used on wounds, it protects the injuries and keeps them clean, by holding the dressings in place and should any fluid pass through the dressing, then it absorbs it. It is a useful alternative to cotton wool because if in contact with a wound its gauze prevents it from sticking. It is essential in every veterinary cupboard and first-aid box.

Fibregee

This is foam covered on either side with a fibre pad. For every day use it is excellent, as it can be machine-washed and then dries quickly. In fact, once it has been

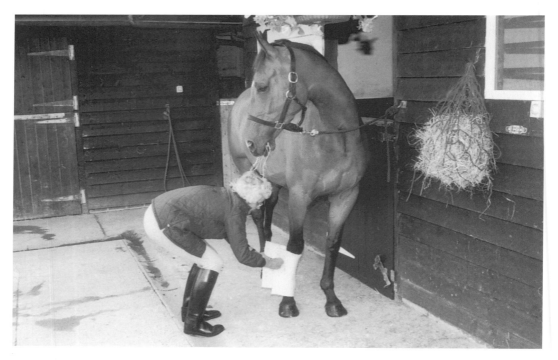

Whether they are used for protection during exercise, or during treatment, bandages should always be applied over a layer of padding to ensure there is no uneven pressure.

washed it is less stiff. Fibregee provides very good protection for travelling, as it can be allowed to extend above the bandages to give protection to the hocks if cut to fit; and it is useful under bandages applied to help keep a horse warm. It should not be applied directly to wounds: for serious injuries that are bleeding or seeping through the main dressing, gamgee should be used (and changed it as soon as it is contaminated).

Bandages

You should have a fairly large selection of bandages.

Stable bandages
Stable bandages are used to keep legs warm and, in some cases, to sevure dressings. If the leg has a surgical bandage on,

sometimes it is wise to put a stable bandage on over the top. A stable bandage is about 5 inches (13cm) wide, and they are made from wool or acrylic. Nowadays it is possible to obtain ones with velcro fastenings, which I find very satisfactory because you can fix the bandage without having to make a knot. This is especially useful because, apart from the convenience, knots can cause pressure damage if they happen to be in the wrong place. If you use traditional stable bandages, make sure the knot is turned under the tape in the area between the tendon and the cannon bone to prevent damage, by pressure.

Surgical bandages
These are crepe. In order to fit correctly they need to be about 4 inches (10 cm) wide. In addition to the traditional type of surgical bandage, which must be secured,

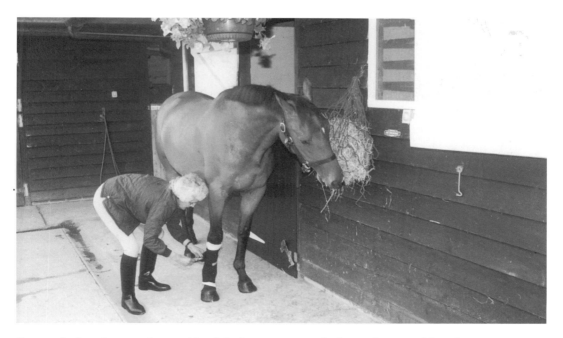

Secure the bandage on the outside of the leg to prevent the horse from catching the tie with the opposite foot.

Bandaging

1. First roll the bandage smoothly and tigthly, starting with the end that will be fastened. Loose bandages are messy and more difficult to apply. If the bandage has an integral Velcro fastening, fold this back on itself to prevent its being caught up during rolling. With the inside of the bandage facing you, wind the bandage towards you.

2. Place the dressing or support around the leg – gamgee in the case of serious wounds, Fibregee in other cases. Always wind the dressing round the leg in the same direction that you will apply the bandage.

3. Hold the bandage in your right hand. Start bandaging from just below the top of the dressing, setting the bandage at a slightly downward angle, so that the top corner of the bandage points up above the dressing. Do not start in the middle of the dressing – as is so often done nowadays – and do not place the bandage outside the dressing as the edge will cut into the leg if it starts to swell. Then start rolling the bandage evenly down the leg, passing the bandage from your right hand to your left behind the leg, overlapping as you go, and all the time maintaining an even pressure.

4. If the fetlock is to be bandaged as well, ensure that the bandage crosses it in the centre at the front, leaving a small inverse V, before going back up the leg. Ensure that the bandage is kept just above the gamgee or Fibregee to prevent pressure on the back of the pastern where the major tendons pass down into the hoof. The skin here is tender and needs protecting from coarse edges. This part of the bandaging is the only section consisting of a single layer, so overlapping is important to ensure the

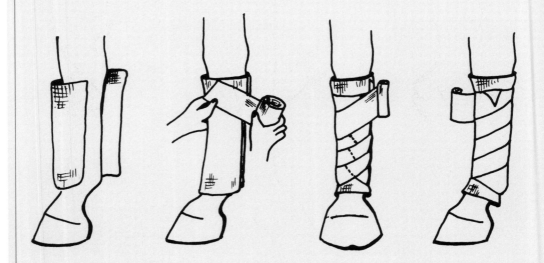

1. Only bandage over padding.

2. Start bangaging below the knee.

3. Continue down to below the fetlock for support.

Bandaging the foreleg.

Bandaging

bandage remains in place. If the fetlock is not to be included, stop just above it and work your way back up to the top of the dressing.

5. When you reach the top, turn down the corner that you left pointing upwards when you started, and pass the last section of the bandage over this turned-down flap to secure it.

6. If the bandage has a Velcro fastening, stick it down, making sure that the hooked surface completely covers the looped surface so that it cannot be accidentally pulled off. If a tape

is used, flatten the tape out to make sure there are not rucks or wrinkles in it, then pass the ends round the leg in opposite directions, crossing them over at the back. Tie the tapes together on the outside of the leg, between cannon bone and tendon. Never tie them at the front or back, or on the inside. Tie the tapes with a full bow, and turn the ends under the tape so that they cannot be caught on anything.

(Continued overleaf)

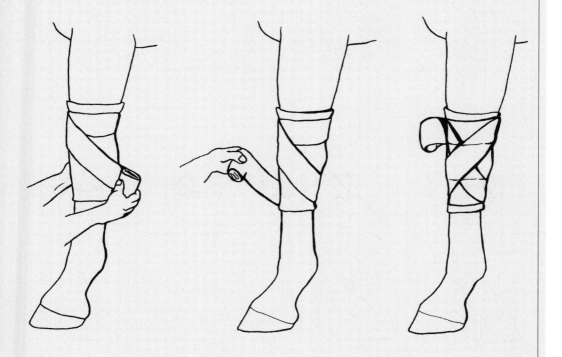

1. Start above the knee joint.

2. Bring the bandage diagonally across the joint.

3. Wrap the bandage around and diagonally back across the knee joint in a figure-of-eight configuration.

Bandaging the knee.

Bandaging (continued)

The bandage should be firm enough to be secure, but you must check that it is not so tight that it stops circulation. It should be applied at a tension of half its full stretch capacity, so that once secure you are able to ease a finger underneath it. The veterinary surgeon will tell you what part of the leg to bandage, and what dressing to apply, but whatever the type of bandage you apply, the principle will remain the same.

Bandaging the hock.

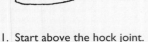

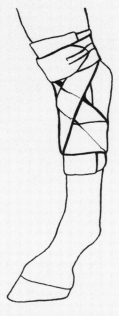

1. Start above the hock joint.

2. Pass the bandage diagonally across the joint and wrap around.

3. Pass the bandage diagonally back up the leg in a figure-of-eight configuration.

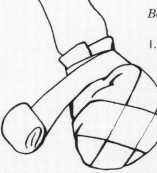

Bandaging the foot.

1. Enclose the foot in padding or heat-retaining material for poulticing.

2. Criss-cross the foot with the bandage to keep padding in place.

For good support, always continue the bandage to below the fetlock.

there are now self-adhesive types. There are also elasticated bandages, but with the modern self-sticking ones, they are less needed, though they still have their uses. Always put the bandage on in the same direction as the padding underneath is wrapped. While it should be tight enough to provide support, too tight is dangerous and can cause more problems; bear in mind that some injuries may result in swelling. Too loose and they will slip down, taking the dressing with them.

Tubigrip
This is an elasticated, surgical, tubular stockinet, normally intended for human use, but extremely useful for holding certain dressings on to legs. The size required depends on the situation of the wound. Tendons and fetlocks require a size to fit snugly, but not tight. You must allow room for swelling. Tubigrip is also

worth keeping for your own use if you should injure a wrist or ankle. Quick action is equally important for you.

Gauze and Lint

You should have a good supply of sterile, non-adherent, absorbent dressings. These take in the extraction from the wound, without sticking to it. Gauze is an open-weave dressing that comes in rolls and packs from which you to make a folded dressing. Lint is another type of close-weave dressing, which also comes in rolls,

> Before using antiseptic dressings, ensure that they are suitable for the patient's condition. It is important not to mix some antiseptics, in case they react unfavourably with each other.

but it has a soft cotton backing (this should be applied gauze side on to the wound). These items do not contain antiseptic dressing, as some special dressings do.

Cotton Wool

Buy large rolls, as you are likely to use fairly large sections – chunks, in some cases, to clean up serious injuries. Never use a piece of cotton wool more than once: dispose of it into a container, and then use a fresh piece for the next wipe. I have found it a great help to keep a sterile container with a lid filled with fairly large chunks pulled off the roll. This saves time wasted in fumbling to remove the next chunk from the roll, prevents the main roll from becoming contaminated and dirty.

In addition to the large rolls, I also use cotton wool balls. These are made from finer, softer, cotton wool, and are suitable for cleaning eyes, as well as for cleaning

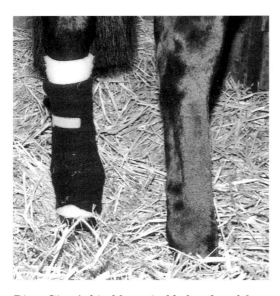

River Gipsy's hind leg suitably bandaged for poulticing, with even pressure and good fetlock protection.

small injuries. These are also kept in a clean container.

Surgical Tape

This is useful for securing bandages. Plastic tape is also used. When using tape, be careful not to restrict a leg if it is swelling.

TOOLS AND EQUIPMENT

Thermometer

This should be of veterinary type with a cap on the top end. Digital thermometers have a wide, flattened section at the end, and therefore do not have a cap. The thermometer must be kept in a protective case to keep it clean.

Scissors

There are three main types.

- One long, sharp-pointed pair for cutting gamgee and other materials (but not for use near injuries themselves).
- One pair of standard size with straight blades and blunt ends, for use on or near a horse.
- One pair of standard size with curved, blunt-ended blades for use on hair or skin that needs to be removed.

Clippers

Every stable should have a pair of small, electric clippers. These should be rechargeable rather than mains connected. You should keep three veterinary blades – coarse, medium and fine. I always believe in clipping the hair back from around a wound to ensure that it is kept as clean as possible and to prevent the injured area spreading outwards through crusted hair. There is also the advantage that you can see the affected area more clearly and are therefore more likely to notice any alterations should they occur. It also helps the hair to grow back the correct colour, without scarring. The odd hairline scar will remain, but the majority do go. I also have an old pair of manual clippers that are slightly coarser. They have all played their excellent part in helping to cure some very nasty injuries.

Twitch

Twitches are used as a means of calming a horse that is apprehensive or in pain. Under the effect of the twitch, the horse will stand stock still and the eyes assume a glazed expression.

There are two kinds of twitch. The traditional one consists of a length of wood

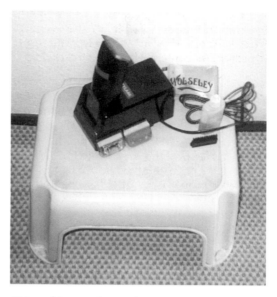

Skin and wounds can be treated more efficiently when the area is clipped. Rechargeable clippers with different blade sizes are a useful asset.

The author applying a twitch to Midday Phlight.

with a hole in one end through which a loop of cord is passed. I always use lamp-wick, which is soft and humane. The loop is placed over the horse's upper lip and the wooden handle twisted to tighten the loop.

The modern twitch is a pincer-like implement made of rust-proof aluminium. This clamps the upper lip and has the same effect as the traditional one.

Twitches appear to work by inducing the release of endorphins, which are the body's natural tranquilizer.

Tweezers

These are useful in various situations, most obviously to a thorn or other foreign body protruding from the skin or hoof.

Syringe

A large-sized plastic syringe is very useful for cleaning out wounds in difficult places. It can be used without anything on the nozzle to pump water or antiseptic lotion either into or over an injury. It takes the place of a hose, when running water is not available. When you do use a hose, ensure that it is clean; a dirty one will introduce infection.

Plastic syringes are also used to administer worming preparations (*see* Chapter 4).

Foal Teat

This is essential for feeding a foal if for any reason the mare cannot do so herself. When such a situation arises, there is rarely time to go out and find one, so it should be kept permanently as part of the veterinary cupboard. Had I not had a calf teat – very similar to but not as good as a foal one – I could never have saved River Gipsy. I had to bottlefeed her until Galavant accepted her and she could suck herself.

Using the Twitch

Twitches are effective and humane when they are used with care and consideration.

1. When applying a twitch, ensure that the lip is folded inwards so that the loop, or clamp, does not make contact with the lip's inner lining.

2. Once applied, wait for a couple of minutes for the twitch to take effect before performing the necessary task.

3. The duration of the sedative effect of the twitch varies from one individual horse to another. In any case it should not be left on for more than fifteen minutes. If necessary it can be reapplied later.

4. When the twitch is removed, massage the horse's upper lip to stimulate circulation to the area.

Sponges

These are essential for cleaning up. Baby sponges and bath sponges are very satisfactory.

Needle and Thread

To stitch bandages and dressings, and so on.

Disposable Gloves

These should be worn when dressing wounds or doing any close contact work on injuries where there is a risk of spreading infection.

The ones that are available in packs from most chemists are perfectly adequate in most circumstances. But for serious cases it is better to use sterile, surgical gloves.

Padding a headcollar.

1. Cut the padding to the correct length.

2. Lace the padding so that it encloses the strap.

3. Slip a retaining bandage (e.g. Tubigrip) over the padding using a card or ruler as a guide.

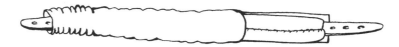

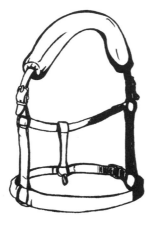

4. The finished article with protective headpiece.

Ice Packs

There are various brands of ice pack and cooling gel, designed to cool off strained legs or reduce swelling. If you are competing it is really wise to keep some. They should be stored in a refridgerator until required. Crushed ice in a plastic bag, or frozen peas, will also work .

Buckets

You should keep two of these specifically for veterinary use, one for containing solu-tions, and so on, for treating the horse, and one for washing human hands. Both must be kept spotlessly clean and disin-fected. You should also have bucket for your horse's feet. For safety, this bucket should not have a handle.

LOTIONS & POTIONS

Witch Hazel

This is a clear liquid that I have found to be extremely useful for bruises and slight strains both for the horse and myself.

Zinc and Castor Oil Cream

This softens the skin and helps surface cuts to heal without scarring. Cuts that are more or less healed will also benefit from it. Warm it slightly before applying to let it soak into the skin. It was the cream that helped River Gipsy's hind legs to recover after having the hair and skin stripped off, from stifle to coronet – it grew back the correct colour, and only one minor scar remained, where the wire had gone deep into the inside of her off hind leg above the hock. I also used it to heal my badly damaged face after River Gipsy collapsed on the road.

White Petroleum Jelly

This is another product that can be used to soothe the skin and heal minor scrapes. it is also an essential lubricant, which should be applied to the thermometer before taking a horse's temperature (see Chapter 5). However, it is not meant for puncture wounds, serious burns, or cuts. Do not use if there is any question as to whether the injury will need stitching or not.

Surgical Spirit

This is necessary to harden skin made tender by saddle sores and girth galls. In some cases it can also be used for cleaning injuries.

Antiseptic

This is used to kill germs in cleaning wounds and equipment. Use diluted on injuries. Antiseptic is available in lotion, spray and powder form. These can be acquired off the shelf, but I have always preferred to get mine from a veterinary practice as they can prescribe brands that are not on the open market. Some also come in creams like Dermobion, a green ointment that can only be prescribed by your vet. It seems expensive, but it comes in a large pot, and when I worked out the price against the other ointment in a tiny pot that my vet had prescribed as a stand by for cuts, it was no more expensive. In the past I have successfully treated mud fever with it; in fact it is the only thing to have conquered this extensive complaint. It heals cuts and other problems needing this sort of treatment. It is well worth having. Hydrogen Peroxide is useful for applying to clean, dried injuries. It is the base ingredient in a number of antiseptics.

Sprays – if your horse will accept them – are very effective for injuries that need drying. I used the purple one while hunting, and at some stages of fighting mud fever. One needs to soak off the scabs every day or so before re-applying. I used a weak antiseptic that lifted the scabs off effectively.

Wound Powder, which looks like flour, is popular, but I do not like it as I have found that it forms a lid on a cut, which then festers underneath, while the edges become crusty from pus seeping out. The only knee injury never to heal properly with the correct colour hair, was the one on my horse, Points, who was treated with powder. Spray is more effective as it will penetrate right into the injury, without clogging.

For your own hands, you should have an antiseptic handwash, which is available in easy-to-use, pump-action bottles.

Liniment

This is an ointment used to relieve the stiffness caused by certain strains. One type of liniment, Stockholm Tar, is a thick, black substance used to cure foot problems. It is also available as a mixture of tar and fibre for packing holes in the hoof.

Salt

This is used as a disinfectant and can be made into a saline solution as an alternative to antiseptic wash (1 teaspoon to 1 pint/550ml boiled water).

Epsom Salts

These are used in a solution to extract poison or foreign bodies embedded under the skin on the hoof or lower leg. It should be used diluted two handfuls ordinary salt and one handful of Epsom salts to a bucket of hot water. Soak for about twenty to thirty minutes at a time. It sucked out the first two gun shot pellets from River Gipsy's fetlock. It is also used in bran mashes on some occasions, to ensure that the horse's bowels are working.

Vinegar and Bicarbonate of Soda

Vinegar is used on wasp stings and Bicarbonate of Soda on bee stings. They are effective on both humans and animals. open box

SUNDRIES

You should keep a supply of kitchen towels and some mild soap for washing hands and some wounds – mud fever needs the skin to be cleaned with mild, pure soap to remove the scabs before treatment.

Addresses and Telephone Numbers

Keep a list of telephone numbers (and where approriate addresses) for your vet, the police, your own doctor, and someone to be contacted in an emergency should other help be needed. Duplicate lists should be kept at your own home and in the stables in an easily accessible place so that anyone can find them in an emergency. I also keep them on a card in my car.

Record Charts

In order to ensure that all vaccinations, worming and shoeing is done on time, keep a chart and/or a record book, showing the dates and any other important details. When your horse is ill or injured, you should also keep a notebook detailing such information as temperature readings, changes in condition, new symptoms, and so on. These notes should form the basis of progress reports to your vet.

FIRST-AID BOX

In addition to the veterinary cupboard, it is essential to have a first-aid box to take with you when travelling, or visiting horses at grass that are away from the stables. Complete first-aid boxes can be purchased, but it is less expensive to make up your own. For this you will need a container – a large sandwich box or, better still a plastic tool box. First clean it and disinfect it (even if it is new) and then fill it with the items you will need most from the above list. All the essentials and any others you feel are necessary. Dressings can be put in a small plastic box and others in plastic bags for protection.

Sterile dressing packs especially useful for first-aid boxes because they are compact and easily carried. They contain the necessary items to clean wounds under sterile conditions, together with an absorbent towel, and a water-repellent paper, sterile 'field', which is a sheet to place under all equipment. Very useful. A local chemist may be able to supply these, along with sterile gloves.

Mark the first-aid box clearly – I mark mine with the letter V – and keep it in an accessible place so that anyone can find it quickly. On the inside of the lid of the box, paste a complete list of phone numbers: you should include those for the vet and any other people that should be contacted in the event of an emergency. These should be written clearly, so that anyone can know exactly what it means. In addition, it is sensible to include any special instructions that might help cope with the horse, i.e. if your horse has any dislikes or nasty habits. Knowing what you are dealing with makes quick action so much easier, and can make all the difference. This is important because there may be times when the owner cannot help, either through absence or through his or her own injuries.

I learnt the need for first-aid boxes the hard way. Back in 1971, when Galavant and I were off to our first BHS Event – something I had longed for – a bus pulled out across the road in front of our horse box. Neither vehicle was hit, but my friend and I could hear Galavant struggling. We both examined her and she seemed unharmed, so we continued, checking at intervals; it was not until we opened the trailer on arrival, that we found the floor and walls covered in blood. Galavant had small hooves, and the near hind had slipped under the partition. In those days, the partition was covered with a metal sheet, and unknown to any of us it was turned down and out on the under side, and had gashed her coronet and (as I later discovered when the cut started to open) taken a slice of the outer wall of the hoof. Had her legs not been bandaged, the damage would have been far worse. Not only did I foolishly have no first-aid box with me – in those days they were not usual, in fact no one had them – but the duty veterinary surgeon had not yet arrived because the event had not started. In fact he was Galavant's own vet, and set to work on her as soon as he clocked in and was told of the accident. The cut had stopped bleeding, and after treatment it was decided that I could, as she was sound, ride – I was there reporting, as far as I can remember, and everyone was so keen, after my long struggle back, that I should continue. I did my dressage out of order, and tried the other phases, but she was not really interested so I withdrew her.

On my return home, I cleaned the cut again and poulticed it. The main problem was that some straw had become wedged in the cut and also in the crack in the hoof. I extracted what I could with my fingers and tweezers after each daily poultice. After about a week we succeeded in getting it clean. Mercifully she had not damaged anything inside the coronet or the hoof wall. With the wound covered, she was able to go out each day, as the paddock was dry.

Once on the mend, she was borrowed by a Thoroughbred stud in the next village to act as a companion for a mare coming back from stud who would not live on her own. Returning in the autumn, having been under her own veterinary surgeon's care while away, it was decided that the time had come to remove the slice of hoof – the wall had grown well, and true, so it was now possible. Then the coronet was also dealt with. In this case it meant slicing off the top, which had formed a lump, and at intervals continued to seep. Once the lump was off, the foot was poulticed for a couple of days until clear. And she was then re-shod.

In due course, the large cavity in her hoof wall was filled, to close up the gap and protect the inside, and she was back to work. By October, she resumed eventing and hunting, and by the end of the winter the hoof was back to normal. In all, Galavant's treatment was a success, but the incident taught me how important it is to have first-aid equipment with you, whenever you are travelling away from home or visiting horses and ponies at grass.

7 Caring for the Ailing Horse

Nursing your horse or pony when injured or sick entails not only treating the problems but keeping the stables really clean to ensure that no additional infection is introduced. It also means providing as high a level of comfort as possible, for the comfortable, contented horse will recover far sooner than one who is stressed or neglected and wretched. An ailing horse must be warm and able to move without restriction from dirty, deep-litter beds. For this reason we will tackle this part first: without a properly maintained box, additional problems will occur.

MUCKING OUT

If a box is kept clean by thoroughly mucking out each morning and skipping out on each visit to the stable during the day, with any wet bedding removed at tea time, the horse will remain much more comfortable and the risk of smell will be reduced. Such regular attention will also enable you to note any changes that might occur between visits, such as extra, fewer, looser or firmer droppings, and to gauge the rate of hay consumption, and so on, all of which may be very significant.

To muck out a box properly, begin by moving the bedding away from one wall. Sweep the cleared section of floor really clean and dry. Note the state of the floor: urine will mark it in some cases, so make a note of anything unusual. Having cleaned that section, remove the dirty bedding and put clean bedding on the cleared

A clean environment is essential for nursing. Early-morning mucking out (River Gipsy, 1994).

floor. Then do the next wall, removing the dirty bedding and putting the clean straw against the first wall. Start at the door and work round until you have cleared and cleaned each wall of the box. To brush the floor clean, push the broom first away from you then towards you to loosen any dirt. To pick up and sort the straw, I use a two-prong pitch (hay) fork, to separate the dry from the wet, so as not to waste or leave wet, but I use a short four-pronged fork to lift the wet bedding onto a sheet or into a barrow – I prefer a sheet. They will both need rinsing after use. Once clean, hang the sheet to dry. Any remaining, more stubborn bits of dirt need lifting out with a shovel and brush.

If I have no where else to treat my horse, I then groom and do any treatment in the box while the floor is clear and clean. It is a good idea to pick out the feet and clear away the debris before you begin grooming. Peel all the rugs off, bar one, to groom (you must not allow your horse to become chilled). Renew any dressings and administer any treatments; then re-rug before doing the legs and feet. Once all treatment is finished, replace the bedding. Start on the clear wall by the door, working in reverse order to that when you were clearing. Bank well up the walls, and ensure the central area of the bed is level on the floor. Add extra bedding, at least a third to a half a bale of straw (standard bale), to give a fresh dry top layer; then put the two-prong fork into the bottom of the bank, lift and then reverse the fork and push back against the wall for security of the bank and smartness. The bed should be 4 to 6 inches (10–15cm) deep, regardless of type, to protect the horse when lying down and to keep the box warm and dry. When finished, sweep up the doorway to leave a clear area between bed and door to prevent slipping when leaving the box, and then sweep up outside. Finally, clean the water bucket and refill. Mangers, too, have to be cleaned, and like buckets, disinfected if there is any risk of infection.

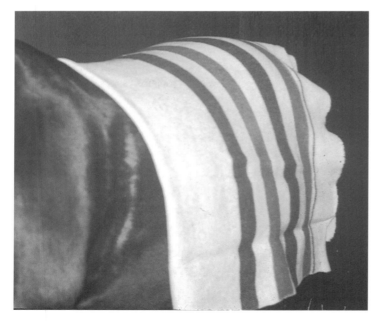

A blanket placed across the loins keeps a horse warm during treatment, or when grooming or clipping.

Caring for the convalescing horse in winter: lots of blankets and plenty of deep bedding.

Types of Bedding

All types of bedding require the same standard of cleaning to reduce smell and dampness. The type of bedding is up to you. I personally do not like shavings, as I find them and even dusty, and they can affect the skin of horses with fine skin. It also sticks to rugs and bandages, not to mention manes and tails, and may also get into wounds.

A horse with respiratory trouble really needs good-quality paper bedding – this must be kept spotlessly clean otherwise it becomes sludge. The first time I saw this used as deep-litter bedding it was appalling mould and sludge draining out by the door. Later I saw it again in an extremely well-run racing stable, where it was fine. There are now many medical beddings on the market. These seem good,

---

Mould

- Mouldy straw is not safe and will trigger off respiratory problems, as will any mouldy bedding.

- Deep-litter beds are very dangerous, for they are normally – I have yet to see one that is not – mouldy under the clean straw in the corners, if not in the centre. When eating their hay, horses will rummage in the bedding in search of any that falls to the floor, pushing their nostrils into the 'danger zones'; then the owner complains when the horse starts wheezing and coughing. Virus infection is one thing when caught by contact, but infection caused by careless stable management is the owner's fault and can in most cases be avoided.

providing they are cleaned out thoroughly each day, although I still use good, dry, clean, wheat straw.

Barley straw is not good, though good-quality oat straw can be all right. Horses can eat it too; it is in many chaff feeds one buys these days. On the whole, if a horse is properly fed, he will not eat the wheat straw, bar the odd bit. Bed-eating can in some cases cause constipation; otherwise you can tell if a horse is eating his bed by how much clean straw has vanished after it had been put down!

Choose your bedding wisely, and if there are problems, consult your vet. Before trying a new, manufactured bedding, it is worth seeking advice in case there is any reason that it might not be suitable for your horse's condition.

STABLING

Heating and Ventilation

We now come to a controversial subject – keeping the stables warm and well ventilated. Boxes vary: some are brick built, others are wooden – those that are fully lined are far warmer than those with only the lower 4 feet (1.2m) boarded. The location of the box is also significant. Those exposed to the full blast of wind are far colder than those in a sheltered position, as the wind – not to mention ice, snow and rain – can rage into the box, soaking and chilling the occupant. For this reason, I do not agree with the argument that the top door of the box should never be shut. An open top door can put a horse at far more risk than if it is

Draught-free ventilation: if necessary, modify the opening of the window, but do not close it up.

shut at night, or during a gale or blizzard; providing the box is well ventilated you are better off closing the top door in these conditions. Bear in mind, though, that only a scrupulously clean box can be shut in. By day the box should be open, except in extreme weather conditions.

Every box must be well ventilated, by which is meant that air should be able to circulate. In most cases, some form of ventilator will be necessary. It must be well above the horse so as not to chill or blow down on the horse. Hot air rises, and this must be let out.

In summer of course, doors are open all the time, except in extreme circumstances like gales, or torrential rain driving into the box. Windows on the other hand, assuming they are open – which they should be, though not all do – are open all the year round. To prevent draughts, they must open inwards with the ends blocked; this blows the air upwards over the horse, rather than downwards into his face and onto his back. This applies to both sick and fit horses, regardless of whether they are Thoroughbreds or tiny woolly ponies. Having the top door open in winter may give more air, and in some respiratory cases help, but it does not prevent colds or influenza. In fact the only case of a cold I can remember was in Castania, who was stabled in a very warm, sheltered yard, in a box with the top door open. Someone else brought in a new horse that had a cold brewing, and without warning us of it put him in a box next to mine. It gave Castania a very runny nose and cough, and within days the entire yard was affected The main thing is to be sensible and, in a case like this, considerate.

One aspect of the design of many of today's stables can cause real trouble without anyone realizing it. Many firms are now making their stables look smarter by filling in the overhang to make a flat roof over the area outside the boxes. Inside the overhang, they leave a wide, long shelf, which is an ideal playground for rats and a home for birds. This shelf is never cleaned out unless the smell of a decomposing animal trapped within the overhang sends the owner in search of the cause. In addition to that, there is a real danger of dust piling up and then blowing down onto the horse below, causing real problems to the lungs, with no one aware of the cause. Dust blows upwards as it is light and then will settle once it can go no higher. In my opinion, the overhang should be open and the walls of the box filled in to the full height. At one of the events I was visiting, I saw one such box, which had the added advantage that the top strip of wood both front and back was hinged to open outwards. This meant that in the summer the front and rear sections of the box could be opened to allow for extra ventilation, while in the winter, the one facing the wind could be kept closed. Should you need to shut the top door at night, then the extra ventilation to the window is an asset. But if you have such a box do ensure you fasten the strip down securely when it is meant to be shut, and fix it when open – horses do not like things bashing against their boxes; it causes them to tense up, and if they are ill this can slow down recovery.

Stable Lighting

When nursing a horse it is really essential to have good, sound lighting. If your horse is ill or injured you can never guarantee that you will not have to administer treatment when there is no natural light.

Protected strip lighting is most satisfactory, but it must be protected, as must all light bulbs, to prevent any glass from accidentally falling into the box – if it ever does, the whole of the bedding must be discarded, and the box thoroughly swept out. If the roof of a box is not suitable for a central light, put in two, one at each end.

This works quite well, but do put them inside the outdoor-type of non-breakable glass cover. Before I covered mine, River Gipsy as a youngster, one night took the bulb out (she had grown more than I realized), and threw it out of the window! I frantically got two covered units and wired them in myself before bedtime. If there is no mains electricity to the box, use a car battery and wire in lights.

KEEPING WARM

A sick horse requires to be kept really warm. In addition to ensuring that your horse's stable is well ventilated but draught-proof, you should keep the horse rugged. The thickness of the rug will be determined by the weather and his condition. If a horse that is already rugged appears cold, add extra. Regulating temperature with very thick rugs is difficult, so I prefer lighter rugs, which can be added to or removed one at a time as required. A sweat rug that is light - such as an Irish-knit anti-sweat rug – is useful as an additional rug between the other rugs to add warmth without weight. I do not care for the old open-weave sweat rugs. Also on the market now are the under-rugs, which have a collar to cover the neck.

To determine whether the rugs are providing enough warmth, slip your hand under the rug at the withers. It should feel warm and dry; if it feels cold and damp, then you will need to dry the horse off by stroking the coat with your hands to stimulate the circulation. When you are doing this, fold only part of the rugs back, and do not remove them. Stroke with both hands, first one, then the other, in a quick, but gentle action to stimulate the blood. Re-cover and do the other side. Normally it is only the shoulders that require this attention, but you made need to massage the flanks. Take care not to chill the patient more – keep away from

> **Checking for Warmth**
>
> To check whether the horse is cold, feel the ears: gently fold your hand around the ear and stroke. If they feel cold, continue stroking until the circulation returns. Add rugs as required.

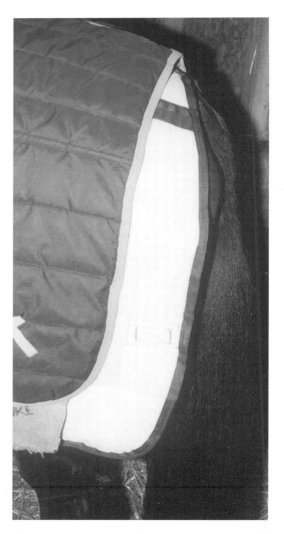

Keeping a horse warm is important, especially when convalescing.

Woollen blankets provide extra warmth, but they must be kept straight to avoid rubbing.

(Below) *A versatile sweat rug can also be used as an extra layer under a stable rug.*

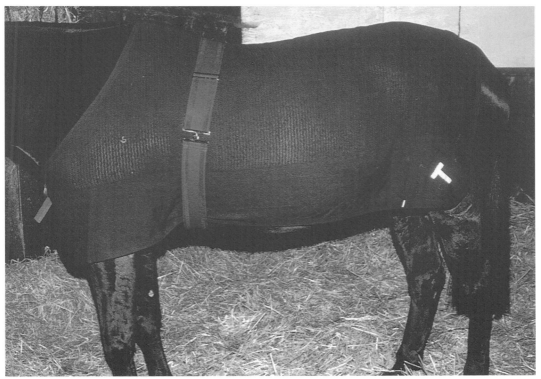

Rugging

1. Regardless of the type of rug you use, fitting a rug is essentially the same. Only the fastening will differ.

2. If you use a blanket with the rug, mark the centre of the blanket to the front and back edges with a pen; this saves a lot of time and frustration because it makes positioning of the rug much easier. To do this, first arrange the blanket in the correct position. Then place the rug in position, ensuring that it is straight and evenly balanced; then mark the position of the withers and the dock on the blanket.

3. To fit the blanket, hold the front in the left hand and the back end in the right hand, and position it well up on the withers, ensuring that your central wither mark is in line with the neck. Smooth the blanket out along the back. Then go to the rear, take the edges of the blanket, and pull it back evenly just short of the tail. The method of lining the front varies. I have found folding the blanket over the withers is best, especially if you are using a roller.

4. Next put the rug over the blanket, placing the front so that the front of the rug is just behind the blanket, so avoiding pressure on the withers. Fasten the front buckle. Check to ensure that there are 4–6 inches (10–15cm) of space between the rug and the windpipe. If a rug is fitted too close to the windpipe, it can affect the horse's breathing. Carefully ease the back end of the rug over the blanket, all the time checking that it remains square.

5. To secure the rug, you have the choice of using a roller (with a pad to protect the withers and spine – *see* opposite), or a cross surcingle. I use the latter with outdoor rugs, but for the horse convalescing indoors I prefer the roller. When using a cross surcingle, ensure the two straps overlap each other about 4 inches (10cm) from the stomach. If it is too loose, it can be caught up on something; if it is too tight it can cause damage to the skin. Carefully adjust the hind leg straps to ensure that they are neither dangling loosely below the hocks, nor so tight that they restrict movement or rub the skin. If you use a roller, put the pad over the spine against the back of the withers (the pad should have a section cut out to accommodate the spine and so keep pressure away from it). Place the roller on top of the pad, so that it lies in the same position as a girth. Check the other side to ensure that the far side is not twisted, then return to the near side and fasten the buckle. It should be quite firm but with sufficient room to place your hand between the rug and the roller.

6. Ensure that the blanket and rug remain smooth and straight.

If required, you can use a blanket with a cotton under-rug with lining for warmth; or a cotton sheet; or, if extra warmth is required, place the blanket between two rugs. Whichever system you use, it is essential that all the rugs and/or blankets fit precisely.

To make a roller pad:

1. *Take a piece of foam that is 2in (5cm) thick, and 1in (2.5cm) wider and longer than the middle section of the roller.*
2. *Carefully cut out a section from the underside of the foam, as shown, to leave a depth of 1in (2.5cm at its centre This will make the foam pad fit more comfortably over the withers.*
3. *Fit the pad under the roller, ensuring that it sits squarely.*

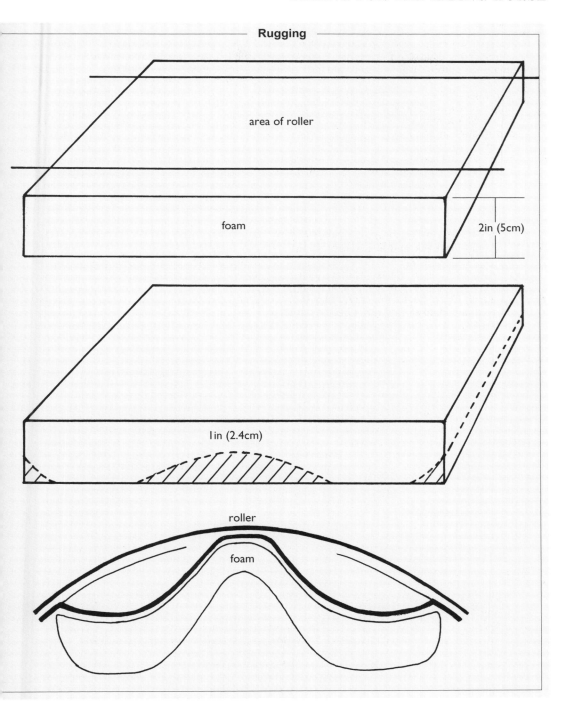

Rugging

area of roller

foam

2in (5cm)

1in (2.4cm)

roller

foam

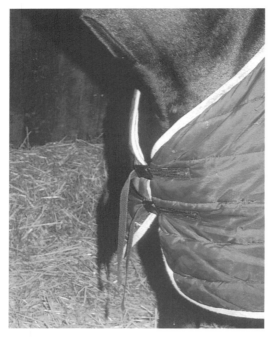

The neckline cut of the rug, and the position of the front buckles, have a significant effect on the comfort of a horse confined to the stable.

(Below) If a roller is used, make sure the spine is well padded.

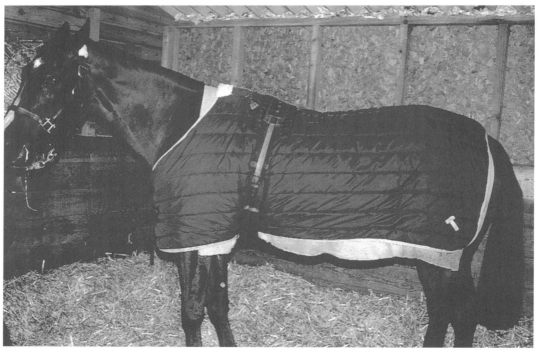

draughts. Once dry, completely re-rug. Remove one at a time, then the last, which should be taken off, shaken and replaced as quickly as possible. Shake each additional rug and replace them one at a time, ensuring they all fit properly – comfort is essential. Should the rug next to the horse's skin be damp, it should be replaced and dried off.

Ensure that the rugs fit well up on the withers and do not press against the chest. The modern cross-surcingles do allow the rugs to slide back, creating pressure on the chest, while a well-fitting padded roller – which is still what I use

except on my turn-out rugs – is more secure. Bandages, too, help to keep a horse warm. Use wool or acrylic stable bandages. Nowadays these are available with Velcro fastening, which is very satisfactory as they do away with the knot and, since the velcro is wider than tape, they reduce the pressure over the tendons. Bandage over either gamgee or Fibregee to protect the legs and add extra warmth. Which you use depends on whether the legs are injured or not. Gamgee is best for wounds, but it must be replaced regularly to keep it clean; unlike Fibregee it cannot be washed (*see* Chapter 6).

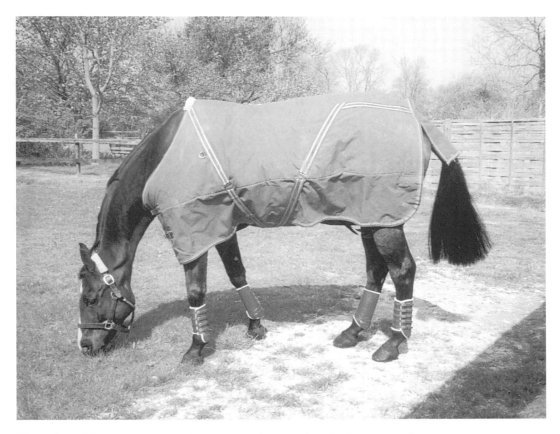

Warmth and leg protection are important when turning the horse out after a period of stable confinement.

The grass species most commonly found in pasture or hay.

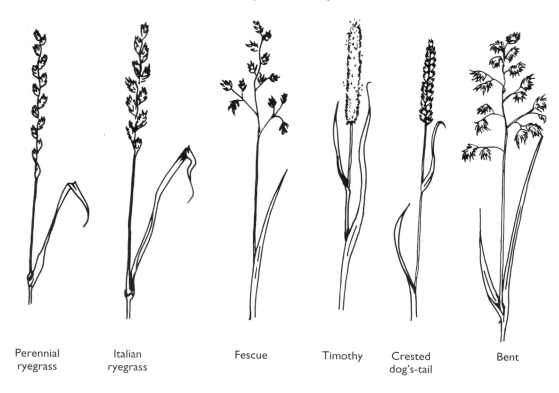

Perennial ryegrass

Italian ryegrass

Fescue

Timothy

Crested dog's-tail

Bent

Legumes most commonly found in hay.

White clover

Chicory

FEEDING

Hay

Hay is the main source of fibre in a horse's diet and very important. It must be top quality, dry, clean, and dust free. There should be no poisonous plants in it – you should always check – and certainly no mould. A bale can appear to be in good condition but, when opened, give off a musty or odd smell; if you have asthma you are likely to detect this immediately; otherwise you should make a point of smelling it to check. If does not have a sweet, clean aroma, either throw out the whole bale, or examine it right through. Sometimes only a tiny part of the bale is affected, and if this section is removed completely – taking a small portion of clean hay on each side – the rest can be used. Dispose of the damaged hay.

It is essential to inspect each section of hay before feeding it. Many people don't, which is time saving but dangerous. Items can be encased within the sections – I have found bits of glass, tin, wire, plastic, even a woolly lamb's leg, all in good quality hay. In

Foreign objects can find their way into hay bales: they can cause serious injury, so always thoroughly examine each section of hay before you feed it.

Fine particles, removed by shaking out the hay, would otherwise cause irritation to the horse's airway.

The haynet tied close to the manger limits the degree of movement required by a horse that is resting from injury.

the case of the lamb's leg, I imagine it was the remains of a fox's kill made while sheep were grazing the land before the hay was made. I always shake up the hay with a two-prong pitchfork, then fill the hay nets. This shaking is important because it helps to remove any dust, and it is far better that it falls onto the hay-barn floor, than on the bedding in the box. Even with the best of bales, it is surprising what one will then sweep up. Never leave discarded hay on the floor, even if the hay store is not immediately adjacent to the stables; clear it out to maintain cleanliness. If you have asthma, wear a dust mask while shaking up the hay.

Not all horses and ponies can eat dry hay, especially not those with respiratory problems. In these cases it is necessary to damp the hay. To do this, many people soak it in a tank or trough of water for twenty-four hours. I cannot see how this cleans the hay. Any dust or fungi – the removal of which is the reason for soaking it – is still there, ready to be eaten as a damp mass of questionable stuff. True the fungi are meant to be killed off, but they are nevertheless eaten. Even soaking in sections for a few hours does not alter matters.

What I have always done is to take a net of shaken hay and place it either on a rack or on a bucket, and then pour either kettles of boiling water or buckets of clean cold water over it, frequently turning the net to ensure that it is thoroughly soaked. In this way, the water can pass through the net, taking any debris with it. If you do this over a bucket, there is the added advantage that you can determine when the hay is clean

Hanging Haynets

1. Ensure that the height of the ring on the wall is such that when the haynet is empty it will not touch the floor. Once empty it should remain high enough to avoid causing a hazard to the horse's feet. At the same time, it should not be lashed so high that the horse has to stretch up to eat; this is uncomfortable for the horse, and will also leave the eyes and nostrils exposed to falling dust.

2. The rope that is threaded through the neck of the net should be sound: there should be no signs of fraying or thinning. Check it regularly. To replace a weak or broken net rope, you can use binder twine (straw-bale string), which can be collected from bales if you cut it at the knot. Take three pieces of bale string and knot the knotted ends together. Hook this end over a hook or door handle, and then plait tightly from top to bottom. (This will take five or ten minutes, depending on your plaiting skills!) Knot the finished plait as tightly as possible to prevent the plait from loosening. Remove the top end from the hook, and make another knot in this top section of the plait. Cut off the original knot about 1/2in (1.5cm) from the new

knot in the plait, so that you are left with plaited twine that is secured at each end by one knot. Then weave the new rope into the neck of the net. Then knot each end of the rope again close to the first knot to form a lock.

3. Fill the net with well-shaken-up hay to the weight required. Pull the rope up tight. The spare rope, coming out of the centre of the front of the net, is then passed through the ring front to back. Hoist the net up high, and pass the end of the rope through the lower part of the net to prevent its dangling too low once empty. Secure the rope to itself just above the neck of the net, fastening with a looped half-hitch (as you would when tying a horse correctly). Pass the loose end of rope through the loop to prevent the horse from untying the knot.

4. If you are hanging a net outside in the field, you must lash it up tightly to prevent its moving about. Pass the rope through several sections of the net and over the fence or other suitable support. Us a net outside only if you are sure it will not present a hazard.

Feeding hay from the floor allows the horse to adopt a more natural grazing position, which is especially valuable for a horse on box rest.

from the clarity of the water in the bucket. You will be surprised at the dirt that comes out into the bucket. I then hang the net up to drain. If there is no where to hang it, you can leave it on an empty bucket until the water has drained out before hanging it in the box, or where ever it is required. By using this method to damp hay, I believe it retains its nutritional value, without going soggy. It stops coughs remarkably well. It also smells nice afterwards, not sour as it can after a long soak. Yes, it is more time consuming, but not much. Should you need to soak a lot of nets, then make a rack to lay them on and then use a hose or bucket – buckets give more force and clean it better in the centre.

If for any reason even soaked or damp hay is unsuitable for your horse, then Horse-hage is a good alternative. It will prevent or at least alleviate the symptoms of allergic respiratory disease. It is excellent for horses in competition work as its nutritional value is high. Like hay it is made from grass, but unlike hay it is left to wilt for less than forty-eight hours before being baled (hay is left until it is completely dry, before being baled), and then the heavy bales are mechanically squeezed to half size to extract the air before sealing in plastic bags. Once open the bale must be used within three days. Never use a bale that has either a cut or a hole in the bag, or mouldy-smelling contents (although this is likely only when the bag is damaged). Haylage is another form of vacuum-packed hay, but since it comes in large round rolls one must have at least three to four horses for it must be used within three days. It is more expen-

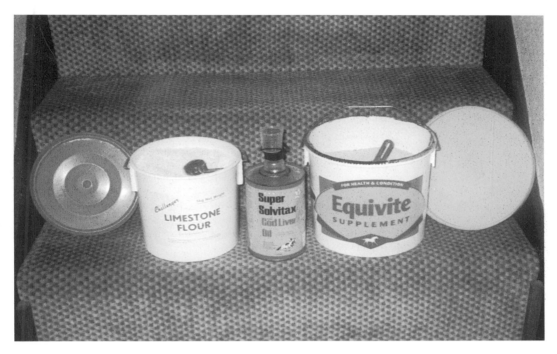

The convalescing horse may require additional minerals and vitamins such as limestone flour, cod-liver oil, or a broad-spectrum mineral and vitamin supplement.

sive than ordinary hay but it is totally dust free and highly nutritious. In addition to these two, there are others.

Regardless of the type of hay or haylage you use, choose the right type for the horse or pony. Ponies require meadow hay or low-protein Horse-hage: while those in active work require a higher protein level. Sick horses need nourishing hay, but those that are very high in protein may be too rich, so consult your veterinary surgeon for advice. I always feed rye-grass hay when I can get it, but I would not feed any hay containing clover, as it is too rich. The main thing is to have sweet hay that will tempt them to eat. Each time you go to check them, remove the net, quickly empty it, re-shake it and return it – it is surprising how they will eat some more! Every bit of attention counts.

Feeds

Fit or sick horses and ponies all need their food. Some owners contend that sick horses do not require anything more than hay, but this is far from true. A nutritional diet is essential to help the patient back to health; a lack of vitamins and minerals will delay healing. Having said this, an ailing horse should not be given 'heating food', i.e., dry oats and other high-grade feeds intended for horses in work. If you have a number of horses in the yard, it is very unkind to deprive the sick or injured one of food if he should wish to eat. It is quite simple – merely make what I call 'false feeds'. In other words, use the basis of a normal feed and add more of it to build up the feed to the quantity required for a feed.

Making a Bran Mash

YOU WILL NEED:

- 1½–3lb (700g–1.3kg) bran (depending on the size of the horse)
- Teaspoon of salt
- Clean bucket with lid
- Boiling water
- A clean tea-towel or other cloth
- Ground limestone flour
- Supplements as necessary
- Cooked linseed (optional)
- Sliced, peeled carrots (optional)

1. Place the bran in the clean bucket and add the salt (which needs to be added to normal feeds as well).

2. Add sufficient boiling water to dampen, but not soak, the bran. Stir until well mixed.

3. Cover with the cloth, and then the lid to keep in the heat. (If the bucket doesn't have a lid, use something else on top of the cloth to keep the heat from escaping.

4. Leave the mash to 'cook'.

5. Once cool (bran mash should never be fed hot), add the limestone flour and any other necessary supplements, and, if the horse likes it, the few slices of peeled carrot. Cooked linseed is also a good extra.

6. Tip into the manger.

Bran mash is a warming feed for the sick or convalescing horse. It aids digestion, and when used with Epsom salts has a laxative effect. Mashes should not be given more than two or three times a week.

Bran mash is a traditional tonic for the horse, but since it changes the gut motility it may adversely affect microbial digestion.

Carrots are a useful appetizer for the convalescing horse. They should be fed washed, topped and thinly sliced, and unless they are organically grown, peeled.

My feeds are all based on chaff and bran – even these days – to which I then add oats and concentrates for fit horses, or just concentrates, depending on what the horse is doing. I then add vitamins and minerals in the form of a wide-based supplement made to provide back up for a normal diet. So with a sick horse off work and confined to his box, I leave out the concentrates and oats, and add extra carrots – peeled is best for those with eating difficulties, while sliced is acceptable if they can eat normally. Apples also add nourishment and will be enjoyed if they are sliced up. The feeds are well mixed while dry and then dampened by adding molasses – one teaspoonful mixed in warm water. In winter I add cod-liver oil (follow the manufacturer's instructions for correct dosage), as it contains the essential vitamins A, D and E, and helps to keep the horse warm. (Be careful not to overdose your horse with cod-liver oil as an excess of the vitamins A and D is toxic.) Because bran lacks calcium, I add ground limestone flour, which has a calcium content of 99.4 per cent.

Loss of Appetite

In formulating a diet for the ailing horse, the main objective is to maintain strength while at the same time keeping the patient happy and content, which is an

83

Linseed

Linseed is the seed of the flax plant *Linum usitatissimum*. It is rich in oils and is highly nutritious. Once cooked, it can be mixed with other feeds, such as bran mash, while the 'tea' and jelly that can be produced by cooking also make useful additives.

- Never feed uncooked linseed, as raw linseed is poisonous and can be extremely dangerous. Hard boiling destroys the toxin.

- To make a linseed jelly, first soak the linseed. Bring it to the boil, and then leave it to simmer until completely cooked. Cooked in this way the linseed forms a jelly which can then be added to feeds.

- You can make linseed tea by adding additional water to the linseed while it is boiling.

important factor in improving a horse's health. Some horses, despite being lame, injured or sick, will happily eat whatever they are offered; others will not or cannot. For the latter type, tiny, very tempting feeds are needed, but these must contain the necessary vitamins and minerals. This is where the linseed helps because it is very palatable, and, if the horse will take a liking to it, glucose. Alfalfa is another useful ingredient that has been found to be very good for laminitis victims. Hi-Fi, a dust-free mixture of alfalfa

Although commercial convalescence mixes are available, some owners may prefer to use straights such as linseed. Linseed must be cooked; it is poisonous in its raw form.

Horses have individual preferences for the texture of coarse rations: choose one that suits.

and chaff, is the recommended way of feeding this. Bear in mind that while the aim is to maintain strength and improve vitality, the horse should not be given oats or concentrates containing 'heating' food.

If the patient will not accept his food in the manger, try offering it in a bucket or scoop, a handful at a time. As soon as one handful has been eaten, offer another. Keep the feed in a bucket placed near by but out of the horse's sight. When Castania was injured the veterinary surgeon had to blister her shoulder; she could not stand for long and she lost interest in her food. I found that if I curled up on the floor beside her, she would eat out of my hand while I talked to her and stroked her. It worked, I kept her going and got her back on her feet. Castania was a very special little mare, I would not have curled up with any other horse. Squat down, yes, as one can get out of the way in a hurry if necessary. At the time it was becoming excessively difficult for me to bend or crouch for more than a second or two, so my sitting down with her was the only option. We

were fighting back together: she had saved me in the accident, and I was not losing her now. Nevertheless I do not advise owners to sit down beside a horse unless they are one hundred per cent sure that the horse is safe – they too could injure themselves and that would be foolish.

WATER

It is vital that horses and ponies have fresh water all the year round, regardless of the weather, and regardless of whether they are healthy or ill. It must be always be clean, and renewed frequently. The bigger the tank, the slightly longer it will last, but buckets require changing twice a day, for healthy horses as well as sick ones. If the sick horse has a runny nose or is dropping food out of his mouth, then the water bucket must be changed more often – it must be kept clean and fresh. Discharge from the nose and semi-chewed food dropped from the mouth will contaminate water and merely increase infection. Running noses

A plentiful supply of fresh, clean water, both in and out of the stable, is essential for horses.

come not only from influenza and colds, but other diseases too. River Gipsy's nose was running the day she died.

After drinking the sick horse or pony will very often remain with his head hanging over the bucket, causing contamination as the discharge drips into the water. For this reason, you should never top up a water bucket; you should always empty it and wash it out thoroughly before refilling. The automatic water systems are not ideal because they are hard to keep free from contamination, and they make it impossible to gauge how much water the patient is drinking. In many cases, the rate of water consumption is very important: too much or too little are both clues

to progress, or lack of it; and in the apparently healthy horse, it may be the first sign that a problem is brewing.

The freshness of the water is crucial: stale water will often discourage the horse from drinking. So, too, will a full stomach – hence the reason for providing fresh water before a feed. In cold weather, it often helps to remove the chill from the water by pouring a kettle of boiling water into a bucket of fresh water. Many horses love it. In bitter weather, I always top-up the bucket with boiling water regardless of whether the horse is sick or healthy. Anything that prevents the horse from becoming chilled is worth the extra time.

8 Accidents ─────────────────

Accidents will occur to the very best of horses and ponies, even if they are well cared for. Some injuries are only minor, while others can be very serious. Injuries that look to be minor on first inspection can in some cases be more serious, which is why it is important to check them regularly. Well cared for horses are less likely to suffer than those left to fend for themselves. Horses are left for days – weeks in some cases – without regular examination. Sadly nowadays, a lot of owners are far too inclined to trust to fate in this way, and their animals do suffer far more than those that are cared for properly.

AT GRASS

Though many accidents occur while at work, exercising or at competitions – including hunting, schooling, racing (on the flat and over fences) – it is often out at grass where many accidents happen. How often in the press we read of some highly talented horse succumbing to trouble while having a rest or just an hour's break in the field. Sometimes they are put out for the season; others may have to be retired or even destroyed. Fit horses love playing around, and injuries can happen there are any sharp edges anywhere in

A tree makes a useful fixture for a haynet in the paddock.

their field – protruding nails on fences, loose or weak wire, weak rails. This is why good paddock management and regular checking of your horses while at grass is so important.

Having said this, even well-maintained paddocks can have potential for accidents. Pieces of metal or glass lying in the grass or buried in the soil can cause serious gashes to the legs and feet. In dry weather, horses may damage their feet or heels on surface hazards; but in wet weather, the feet may sink into wet soil and come into contact with buried objects. They have only to tread on a corner and the whole object can come up, turn over and cut into the fetlock, as well as the foot. This once happened to Galavant while in foal and out for her daily spell in the paddock. Owing to heavy rainfall the ground was very muddy in places, and when I brought her in from the field it was necessary to clean her legs. This process revealed some severe cuts to the lower leg and foot, which needed immediate attention.

Once again, this incident demonstrates the value of vigilance and good stable management. Turning a horse straight from the field into the stable without so much as a cursory glance can mean missing something important. Swift discovery and prompt application of the necessary treatment will guard against infection and scarring, and often save pain and heartache in the long run.

As the cuts had to be kept dry, Galavant was unable to be turned out again until the spring. She was too lame to be ridden but needed some exercise, so I led her out twice a day around the village and surrounding lanes, with odd stops for short grazing bouts. Since mares in foal must be

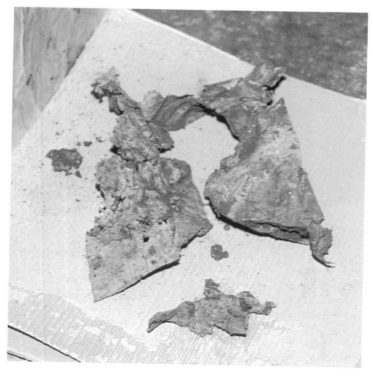

A jagged piece of metal hidden under the soil caused serious damage to Galavant's hoof in December 1976.

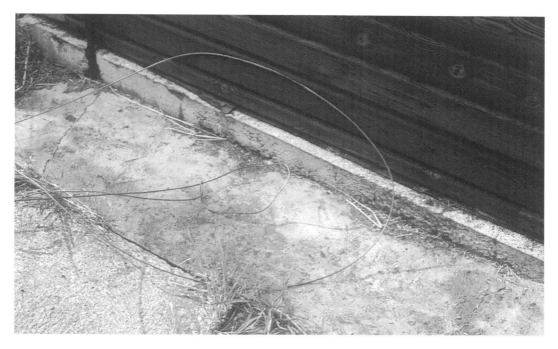

A stray wire is always a danger to the horse's legs. This fence wire was removed from River Gipsy's leg.

exercised gently, this routine suited Galavant very well. I used a lungeing cavesson with a lungeing rein attached to the centre ring to give me control. I later found the cause of her injuries – a piece of rusty, corrugated iron. The bulk of it was deep in the ground, but a large portion had surfaced as a result of the wet conditions.

Unfortunately people have a habit of throwing tins and bottles over fences, so it is especially important to walk the boundaries of your paddock regularly, removing any hazards you may find. Any protruding nails must be hammered in or pulled out. Wire should be tightened or replaced. Even a sound fence can be broken in an accident.

A few years ago River Gipsy was turned out in a paddock adjoining another containing two of my friends' horses. One of the horses, a gelding, became so enam-

oured with Gipsy that he decided to push his way through the wire fence to join her. One strand broke and sprang out to cause a freak accident. Mercifully, I was just checking them as it happened; the loose wire somehow lassoed River Gipsy's off foreleg above the knee, and she fell backwards down the hill, pulling about thirty feet of wire out. I caught her immediately and managed to loosen the wire enough to free her leg.

Externally the cuts seemed to be only surface injuries (but in fact they were quite deep under the skin), and she had gone into shock. Unfortunately she also seriously injured her back and had a problem standing on her off-hind leg. Luckily, the stable was at the bottom of the paddock and I managed to entice her to walk down to it. I left her resting for a couple of

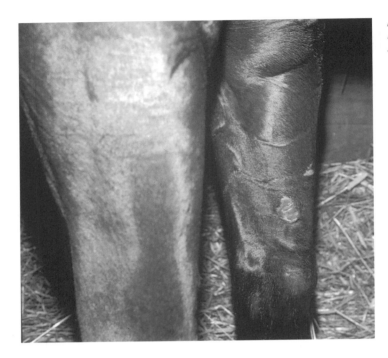

Straight wire can cause lacerations even though the skin may not be broken.

hours, but the stress just left her standing, dozing in her box. She ate a bit in the evening, but I felt she had not recovered satisfactorily by the morning and the vet was summoned. Antibiotics were prescribed for the cuts, and her back was worked by a chiropractor, who gave her a course of treatment to enable her to move more easily. River Gipsy was stabled for several days before being turned out again. How the wire formed a figure of eight around her leg, we will never know. Had I not been inspecting the horses at the time of the accident the injuries could have been more serious, which again underlines the importance of making regular checks on horses at grass.

Vandalism is another cause of injury, and regrettably it is on the increase. When she was eighteen months old, River Gipsy was attacked in her paddock and driven into a solid fence. She brought it down, stripping the skin off both her hind

legs, from stifle to coronet, in the process. It took time, but eventually all the hair grew back and it was the correct colour. Eighteen months later, River Gipsy was shot obliquely across the head and shoulder while away from home. Over the years we extracted a vast number of pellets (over 180), fifty of which came out of her head. Every inch of her body was covered. The damage, both in lead poisoning and mental trauma, took a long time to repair.

ON THE ROAD

Accidents while at work can occur both on the roads and on agricultural land. Road accidents can generally be divided into two main categories. In the first the horse simply trips up, or slips, and falls down, normally on the knees, though some go right down. This can cause some very serious gashes and bruising to the

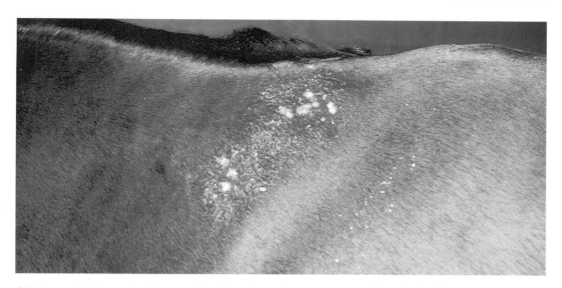

Shotgun pellets eventually emerging from deep tissue two years after the incident. River Gipsy, 1984..

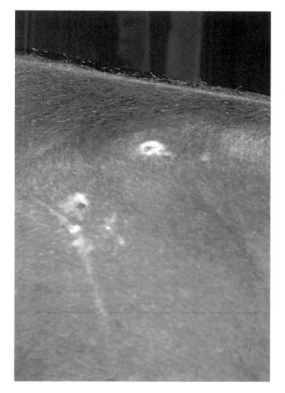

(Left) *Further shotgun pellets were still being eliminated from the body in spring 1985.*

(Above) *Ten years after the original incident, a single shotgun pellet emerges from River Gipsy's right foreleg.*

knees – and certainly minor injuries – in addition to cuts and bruising to any other areas that hit the ground. The odd horse will even fall, roll, and then lie still; but in some cases, if the rider can stay on, it is possible to induce the horse to stand up by using legs, hands and body.

Worn shoes are frequently responsible for bringing a horse down on the road. I recall one occasion when I took Galavant hunting. Her shoes were becoming smooth, but the farrier had been unable to shoe her before the meet, and foolishly I decided to go anyway. At one point, we came from cross-country on to a road, and poor Galavant lost her grip on the road's smooth surface and slipped over sideways. We both had cuts and bruises, although I was nonetheless able to hack home. After this incident, Galavant became very prone to stumbling and slipping up as she came off grass on to tarmac, and then rolling on me.

Traffic is the other cause of serious accidents, and these are frequently fatal. Cars, lorries and motorbikes often show little regard for horses on the road. In a few cases accidents cannot be avoided, and sudden noise or movement from such as birds and dogs will distract drivers or make horses shy. Castania was involved in a serious road incident on a byroad. She was rammed once in front, and then, after I had turned her to escape, rammed three more times from behind. The last bang was so hard that it knocked me out and I lay slumped between her ears. Coming round I slipped off and stood with my hand up, between my horse and the still oncoming car. The driver stopped just

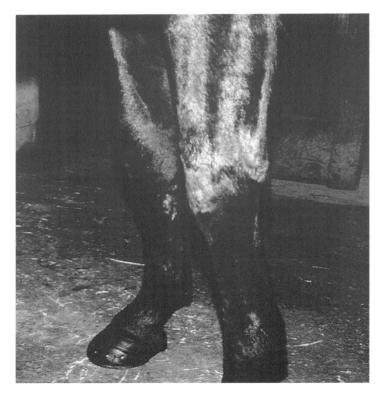

A swelling may not appear until some time after the accident that caused it. This is River Gipsy's leg a few days after the road accident.

River Gipsy's right foreleg had sustained an arterial cut.

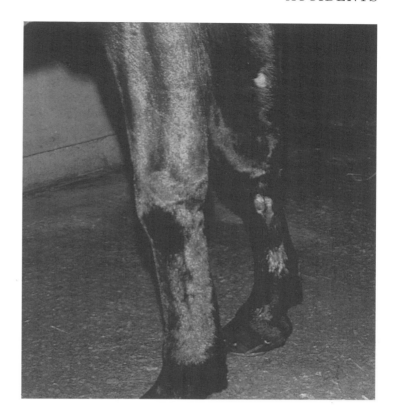

short of my feet and my stomach. I had been tight against the bank and was prepared for the car to break my right leg; however, it was Castania who was hit, on her left leg. The injuries were extensive to us both, but it was some weeks before the full extent of the damage showed up.

In the early 1980s, River Gipsy contracted a virus that caused anaemia. This led to a serious accident when she collapsed head first onto the road. I was thrown off, gashing the side of my face along the tarmac, even under the straps of my crash helmet. Poor Gipsy was injured too; her hind legs, knees, fetlocks and off-fore tendon were all cut. Mercifully I had a friend with me who was able to attend to my horse while I sought help and someone else bandaged her legs to stop the bleed-

ing. I telephoned the vet, who was immediately able to attend to River Gipsy. She was prescribed box rest for the next seven weeks, and by the end of some intensive nursing the scarring was minimal.

The results of treatment were far less satisfactory in the case of my horse, Points, back in the 1950s. We were making our way down a hill by the side of the road when she stumbled and fell into a pile of stones and nettles, badly cutting her knees. The vet treated her knees with wound-dressing powder. They healed, but the area was left with indents and the hair regrowth was white. Thereafter, I have never used wound-dressing powder. It may be quick to apply but it is not the most effective treatment in my opinion (*see* Chapter 9). It forms a dry crust under which pus is able to build up and burrow back into the wound, making the indent worse.

CROSS-COUNTRY

While accidents that occur when in action across country are similar to many others, there is the added complication that they are usually done at speed, causing the horse and rider to hit the ground with considerable force. This can result in broken bones and sometimes death. Racing seems to be one area of equestrianism that has its fair share of trouble. If more than one horse falls, many others can get kicked and injured. Backs can also get strained, though it is amazing how many get away with it, as they are fit. Tendons are another target for strains. Even hacking across country or along lanes can cause problems if your horse shies or bolts.

IN THE STABLE

Casting is one of the most common types of stable accident. Casting is the term used to describe a horse's rolling over on the stable floor and becoming stuck with his legs jammed tight against the wall. If the horse is sensible, he will just lie there; but if he panics he will struggle and kick, injuring himself in the process. Casting may occur either because the horse is simply inclined to roll, but it may also happen when a horse rolls in his attempt to relieve the pain caused by colic.

The sooner a cast horse is found the better. The longer the horse is down, the more damage may be done. On first finding a cast horse, assess how he is lying. If he has a good bed, banked correctly around the wall, there is a chance that you may be able to manoeuvre him round and away from the wall by pulling the tail, as this kind of bedding will allow him to slide. However, if this is not the case, other methods will be needed.

Mangers can also cause problems, as the odd horse will insist in putting his front hooves in the manger and then getting them stuck. There was one horse I remember who belonged to a friend and was always being found trapped. I helped to release him a few times. We had to lift one hoof up first, so that he could lift the

---

Uncasting a Horse

1. If you have help, get one person to kneel on the horse's head (avoiding the eye) to keep him steady and stop any struggling.

2. Place looped rather than tied ropes, over the hind and fore foot that are nearest to the floor. A third rope on the headcollar is also helpful if an assistant is available to hold it. If necessary, lungeing lines can be used as a substitute for ropes.

3. The person restraining the horse's head should get up and, standing well back to allow room for the horse's legs to come right over, you and your assistant can then start to

pull evenly on the ropes. With luck, the horse will roll over quickly.

4. As soon as the horse is facing away from the wall, drop the ropes and give the horse space to get to his feet; once they can move their legs out and sit up, they can get up. But be careful not to cause further trouble by forcing them up too soon.

5. Bear in mind that the horse may be unsteady and frightened at this stage, so approach carefully to examine him for any injuries or problems. If in any doubt, telephone the veterinary surgery for advice.

Haynets should be securely tied, well above the reach of the horse's forelegs.

other himself and then pull sideways. I remember on one occasion when another horse was found with a hoof stuck in a metal hay rack. Mercifully, a groom managed to release it, unharmed, by prising the rack bars apart.

Horses, as you can see, can do silly things. Haynets must be hung correctly (*see* Chapter 7). When empty a net should be well clear of the floor to guard against legs or hooves becoming entangled, which can cause serious stress and strains to the horse's legs. Water buckets and mangers must not have any sharp or protruding parts. If you use buckets for water, make sure they are the heavy, flat-bottomed type that are not easily tipped over, and that the handle lies flush with the bucket rim. (Handles should always be turned towards the wall where they will not be caught in a horse's leg.)

Some horses have a habit of kicking the stable walls, cutting, bruising and jarring their legs in the process. This can also damage the stable, and if it is not of solid construction the horse may injure himself more seriously.

Never leave stable tools, such as forks, shovels and brushes, in your horse's box as these can also cause damage. Badly fitted rugs can also cause stupid accidents. If leg straps and cross surcingles are used ensure that they are not left too loose, as this can put the horse at risk of catching a leg, especially when lying down.

POISONING

This is a threat that can largely be overcome with careful management. The main precaution that you can take is to be extra careful not to turn your horse or pony out anywhere within reach of trees, plants or substances that are known to be poisonous. There is a number of poisonous plant species that you should be familiar with and take steps to avoid.

The poisonous plants that you are likely to come across will vary according to the

---

Lead Poisoning

Lead poisoning can be very serious. In the past, paint was based on lead and caused untold harm when ingested through licking or chewing doors. Nowadays, lead paint is not generally used, but lead can remain toxic for many years, and it is still found in roof tiles, shotgun pellets, fishing weights, and car batteries. Use only unleaded paint on stables, and in any other places accessible to a horse or pony. Ensure there are no pieces of roofing, lead-sheeting or old tins of leaded paint, or similar materials left around. Sometimes substances surface without anyone knowing they were there, so it pays to keep the areas around buildings clean and tidy, grass cut down and raked up, so that unwanted objects can be detected before they cause harm.

---

area you live in, although many species are widespread and may appear almost anywhere.

Yew – the most poisonous tree in Britain – is widely planted in hedges and churchyards. Every part of the green, spiky-leafed tree is poisonous, and even tiny amounts can be fatal. Never let your animals anywhere near it. Even the wind can blow bits quite a long way. When riding past a yew tree, be prepared for your horse to try to nip a piece off. Should he do so, waste no time in extracting it from his mouth before it is swallowed. In such circumstances, speed is vital. Use the bit to lever the mouth open . Although this sounds rather barbaric, such an occasion warrants immediate action; and providing the bit is of good quality, no damage should be done.

Also common in garden hedges are Privet, and Box. Be careful never to let trimmings anywhere near equines.

In wild hedgerows and woods, you might come across Deadly Nightshade, which as its name suggests is a highly poisonous plant, as are its relatives, Bittersweet (or Woody Nightshade) and Black Nightshade. Other dangerous plants that are typically found on roadside banks and in woods and hedgerows include Charlock, Bryony (both Black and White varieties), Hellebores, Thorn-apple, Lily of the Valley, Aconite, and Foxglove.

In parks, gardens and open fields, the magnificent Oak provides a valuable source of shade in summer, but its leaves and acorns are both poisonous. It is in the autumn that the greatest risks occur, when the acorns first fall to the ground, unripe. Some horses take a fancy to them. Dry ground puts horses more at risk because the acorns are easier to pick up; and if there is lack of grass, other forage tempts the horse. If the ground is wet then use a roller to force the acorns into the ground, which will reduce the risk of horses eating them.

Some plants poisonous to horses.

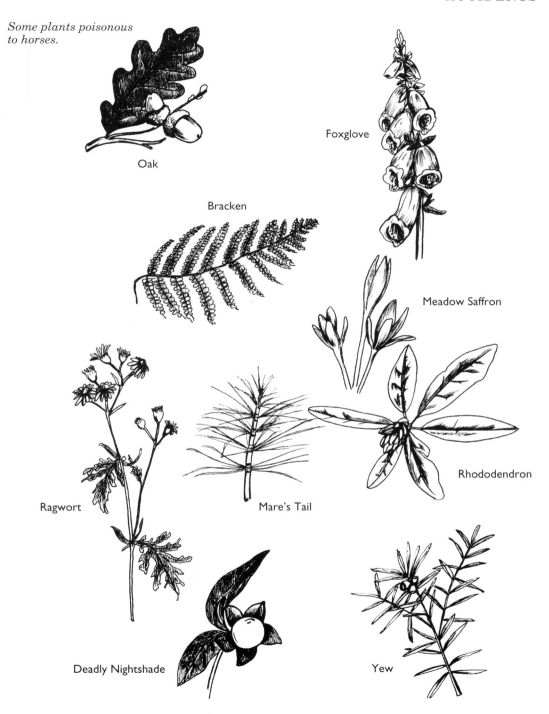

Oak

Foxglove

Bracken

Meadow Saffron

Ragwort

Mare's Tail

Rhododendron

Deadly Nightshade

Yew

The very beautiful yellow-flowered Laburnum is poisonous in all parts. To be safe, it must be as far from the stables and paddocks as possible, preferably with a house or other building between it and the horse's environment. Even so check after a strong wind check that leaves and petals have not been carried into the vicinity. Laburnum is not as deadly as yew, but in large amounts it can be fatal.

Other garden trees, shrubs and that should be avoided are the Rhododendron, Azalea, Kalmia and Cherry Laurel, Avocado and Lupin. The Horseradish plant is dangerous to the horse as it can cause acute inflammation of the stomach followed by death. The Castor Oil Plant can contaminate feeding stuff with castor seed; either in its country of origin or while in transit.

In meadows, rough grassland, and some gardens, Horsetail, of which there are several species, is quite common. Meadow Saffron, Purple Milk-vetch, St-John's Wort, Spear Thistle, Creeping Thistle, Broad-leaved Dock, and Curled Dock are all poisonous meadow plants. St John's Wort is particular remains toxic once it is dry in hay. Hemlock and Cowbane (sometimes called Water Hemlock), are extremely dangerous, as is Hemlock Water Dropwort. Several varieties of buttercup are poisonous, some types more than others. Ground conditions can alter their toxicity: once dry in hay, buttercups are harmless; Creeping Buttercup and Celery-leaved Buttercup are the most dangerous when fresh.

Common Ragwort is the meadow plant that is perhaps most familiar to horse owners; and with good reason, for it is the most seriously dangerous plant growing at random in fields and on roadsides and tracks. In the UK, it is officially deemed to be an injurious weed, and is specified in the 1959 Weeds Act, which means that its clearance from land can be ordered (the owner of the land being responsible). Ragwort has pure yellow, daisy-like flowers clustered in branches at the top of the main stems, and lobed, ragged-looking leaves. It is not instantly fatal. Animals (it is poisonous to all livestock) will graze it over a few weeks before its effects become obvious: lethargy, depression and abdominal pain. As the effects of Ragwort are accumulative you may not notice the symptoms of poisoning for some weeks, by which time it is too late. Thus, it is especially important to be vigilant, checking animals at grass regularly and never turning them out in a paddock that has not been thoroughly checked for poisonous plants beforehand. Once cut or dried, Ragwort is even more dangerous because in hay, silage or dried grass, it is more palatable and therefore more likely to be eaten. In the field, there is only one course of action, and that is to dig each plant out, being careful to remove the roots, before it seeds. All animals must be removed until the process of clearing the field is completed. Once you have dug up the Ragwort, dispose of it by burning, or put it in a plastic bag for garden refuse collection. Do not put it on the muck-heap, or bury it in the ground, or dump it on the roadside.

Bracken, which grows on moorland and other similar types of land, is well known for its poisonous characteristics. Many years ago, it was sometimes used in bedding, but now you are most likely to come across it while out riding or in paddocks. Though wild ponies seem sensible and avoid eating it, domesticated ones are not so discerning, so you cannot rely on their common sense.

Never feed hay, silage or dried grass without checking for harmful plants (especially Ragwort and St-John's Wort), and any other objects. Picking it out will not suffice: you must discard the whole portion. Care must also be taken not to allow your animals access to mouldy products as these can sometimes contain toxins produced by mould fungi and may cause seri-

Poisonous Plant Species

Aconite (*Eranthis Hyemalis*)	Henbane (*Hyoscyamus niger*)
Avocado	Horseradish (*Cochlearia armoracia*)
Azalea (*Rhododendron* species)	Horsetail (*Equisetum arvense*)
Bittersweet, also called Woody Nightshade (*Solanum dulcamara*)	Kalmia (*Kalmia* species)
	Laburnum (*Laburnum anagyroides*)
Black Bryony (*Tamus communis*)	Laurel (*Prunus* species)
Black Nightshade (*Solanum nigrum*)	Lily of the Valley (*Convallaria majalis*)
Box (*Buxus sempervirens*)	Lupin (*Lupinus* species)
Bracken (*Pteridium aquilinum*)	Meadow Saffron (*Colchicum autumnale*)
Broad-leaved Dock (*Rumex obtusifolius*)	Oak (*Quercus robur*)
Calico Bush, *see* Kalmia	Potatoes
Castor Oil Plant (*Ricinus communis*)	Privet (*Ligustrum* species)
Celery-leaved Buttercup (*Ranunculus sceleratus*)	Purple Milk-vetch (*Astragalus danicus*)
Charlock (*Sinapis arvensis*)	Ragwort (*Senecio jacobaea*)
Cowbane (*Cicuta virosa*)	Rhododendron (*Rhododendron* species)
Creeping Buttercup (*Ranunculus repens*)	Sheep Laurel, *see* Kalmia
Creeping Thistle (*Cirsium arvense*)	Spear Thistle (*Cirsium vulgare*)
Curled Dock (*Rumex crispus*)	St-John's Wort (*Hypericum* species)
Deadly Nightshade (*Atropa belladonna*)	Thorn-apple (*Datura stramonium*)
Foxglove (*Digitalis purpurea*)	Hemlock Water Dropwort (*Oenanthe crocata*)
Groudsel (*Senecio* species)	White Bryony (*Bryonia cretica*)
Hellebores (*Helleborus* species)	Yew (*Taxus baccata*)
Hemlock (*Conium maculatum*)	

ous illness. People who like to add potatoes to their horse's feed should be aware that they are hazardous when eaten in a raw state. The dry, green stalks are especially poisonous, as are green or sprouting potato tubers. Once boiled, potatoes are safe, providing the water is thrown away. I would never feed horses with potatoes that are not fit for human consumption.

Paddocks that become saturated during the winter, then dry out on the surface in the spring, only to grow again as soon as any length of rain falls, provide conditions that encourage buttercups and many other poisonous plants to grow prolifically. Buttercups in particular shoot up sharply in a tender state, which makes them more tempting to eat and also more dangerous. If your paddock has buttercups, you must identify their type. If they are found to be either Creeping or Celery-leaved, the application of weed killer might be necessary, although not ideal. If weedkiller is used, keep the animals off the paddock for about a month. If stabled in the field, take them away while it is being done, and shut the doors to keep it away from anything they might come in contact with. Weedkillers are in themselves, another serious cause of poisoning, so in trying to eradicate one source you must be careful not to introduce another.

Symptoms of Poisoning

Symptoms of poisoning vary according to the plant or substance ingested, and range from the fairly mild to the severe and dramatic; the effects of a poison may be instant (as in Yew) or cumulative (as in Ragwort). However, there are a number of signs that should, in the absence of any other immediate explanation, lead you to suspect poisoning and investigate further. Depending on the nature of the substance, poisoning may cause various degrees of damage to the liver, the heart, and the respiratory and circulatory systems. Some of the symptoms of these are listed below.

- Respiration slow and shallow, or distressed

- Noisy breathing and difficulty swallowing

- Abnormal pulse: irregular, weak, fast, slow

- Abnormal temperature

- Muscular weakness

- Glazed expression; eyes partially closed

- Head drooping and frequent yawning

- Pressing of the head against a wall

- Lethargy

- Depression

- Sleepiness

- Muscle tremors, twitching, spasms

- Convulsions

- Compulsive, aimless walking

- Unstable gait

- Staggering

- Paralysis of the hindquarters

- Skin swollen, hot and inflamed, especially muzzle and coronary band, and in white-haired areas

- Sweating when at rest

- Excessive salivation

- Loss of appetite

- Uneaten food retained in the mouth

- Weight loss

- Colic

- Dark-red urine

- Constipation

- Acute diarrhoea

- Instant collapse and death

More than one symptom will be present, but if you are in any doubt as to whether your horse or pony has consumed a poisonous plant or substance contact your veterinary surgeon immediately. Speed can save a life in many cases.

9 Injuries ─────────────────────

Injuries can occur without warning, so it is essential always to have a full veterinary cupboard, and a first-aid box. The first-aid box should be clearly marked so that anyone can find it in the event of an accident, and it should also contain a list of emergency contact numbers (*see* Chapter 6).

In some very serious cases, treatment of an injury may meet with little success or may result in long-term damage; but there is much that the owner can do to increase the chances of healing and a full recovery. As with all illness and injury, co-operation and understanding between owner and vet is what really counts and leads to good results.

BLEEDING

Bleeding can be very serious. The nature of the bleeding will depend on its source: from a vein it will trickle out, but from an artery it will spout out fast, like a fountain. The former can be stopped fairly easily by pressing a pad against the wound, while the latter, especially if it is the main artery above the knee, or for that matter inside the hind leg, needs a tourniquet.

I shall never forget back in 1952 when the local pony clubs had been invited to Porlock by the late Tony Collins to watch the Three-Day Event Team in training for the Olympics. The horse ridden by Bertie Hill (Olympic rider for a long time and the trainer of many riders) stepped on to the dressage arena when without warning the wooden rail snapped and a piece flew

---

The Tourniquet ─────────────

- A tourniquet is only of any real use if the injury is to the leg.

- The tourniquet is an emergency measure, and should not be applied unless the bleeding will not stop with normal pressure.

- The tourniquet works by preventing the circulation of blood from the heart to the injury, so it is crucial that the tourniquet is released every fifteen minutes until help arrives; if the circulation is cut off for too long, death of the limb will ensue.

Applying a tourniquet

1. Use any form of strap, tie or scarf – whatever is to hand – and tie it tight above the wound, i.e., between the wound and the heart. This will slow the blood pumping from the heart to the wound

2. Apply a pressure bandage: place a pad over the wound and bandage it quickly.

3. Send for help with all speed.

---

upwards into the inside of the horse's hind leg. Within seconds the rider was off, and the wood was pulled out and replaced by his fist, which he used to stem the bleeding. He saved the horse in a remarkable manner. In the Stockholm Olympics his

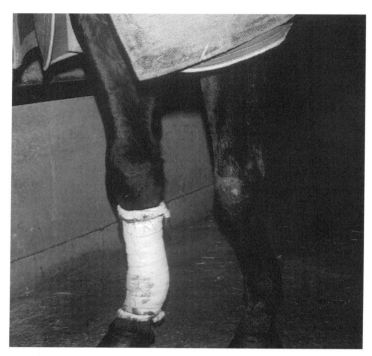

River Gipsy's wound covered with a non-stick dressing under a layer of gamgee and a self-adhesive bandage.

(Below left) *When Galavant's new hoof began to grow, the damaged horn could be removed.*

(Below right) *The horn defect was thoroughly cleaned and filled to prevent further cracking.*

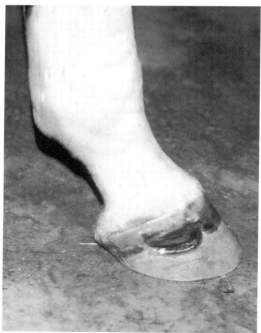

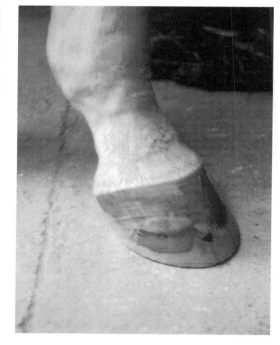

horse got caught on the top of a very nasty fence, and, as before, he was off with speed and lifting the horse back off the top, unhurt. They jumped the fence and went on to win a gold medal with his team. Quick action is what is needed.

Once wounds have bled and dried, then it is safe to remove the congealed blood. Bathe it off using either an antiseptic wash or hydrogen peroxide (diluted one part to 20 parts water), carefully applied with cotton wool. Dried serous fluid – the watery fluid discharged by a wound – can also be removed the same way. If left, both blood and serous fluid will cause scars.

WOUNDS

Injuries come in different sizes and degrees of severity. Bear in mind that 'small' does not necessarily mean 'minor', so all wounds, regardless of their size, should be investigated. The owner can treat minor wounds, but if you are in any doubt you should telephone your veterinary practice for help or advice. Even if you feel confident about treating an injury, you should not continue treatment for more than three or four days if there is no marked improvement. Special treatment may be required, and delay can allow a minor injury to become a more serious one.

Incised Wounds

Incised wounds – cuts or scratches – are caused by a sharp object, such as a piece of metal or broken glass, or a nail protruding from a fence or wall. Many such cuts and scratches are superficial in that they do little more than break the skin; but others, while appearing to have done little or no damage at all, can cause quite deep, serious injury. These do not surface for a few days, when the skin dries off and then peels, leaving a septic cavity.

The first course of action is to clean the wound with an antiseptic wash – I use a saline one, made up of one teaspoon of salt to a pint of boiled water. The wash should be allowed to cool to blood temperature, and then applied with cotton wool. When all the dirt has been removed, you can administer either an antiseptic spray or cream, though some people still favour a powder; I find they clog the wound too much. In the old days there were no sprays, so powder had to be used for drying.

At the outset, regardless of the size of the wound, I always cut or clip the hair off over and around the damaged area. This not only allows you to see the wound more clearly but it also prevents hair-matting, which can result in an extension of the injured area.

The wound should be re-dressed every day. If in a day or two the skin starts to peel off or is seen to be crinkling up, take extra care to ensure that no trouble is brewing underneath. Gently remove the top layer of skin. If the area is 'flat' and healthy looking, then carry on with the same treatment. But if it looks yellowish or appears soggy, call for advice. The patient may require antibiotics.

Never re-dress a wound without first recleaning it. It is important to remove any new dirt that might have settled on it, but cleaning will also remove scabs from the healed area, so that hair can regrow correctly. If you are not already using it, cream is needed at this stage to keep the skin surface soft so that the wound can heal without the skin's being pulled at the edges through shrinking.

Jagged Wounds

Jagged wounds – or lacerations – are tears rather than cuts. Like the small cuts discussed above, these wounds can also be sustained in a variety of ways – when a horse catches himself on a piece of barbed wire or protruding nail, for example, or falls against stone. As a rule, lacerated wounds are far more serious than incised wounds, and it is wise to call for help straight away. Antibiotics are almost certainly required and, if necessary, a tetanus injection. (If the horse is correctly vaccinated, this should only be required when the vaccination's expiry date is approaching.)

Having called for help, and while waiting for attention, clean the area around the wound using a hose or wash, depending on the cut. Then apply an antiseptic, non-stick dressing secured with gamgee and a bandage. At this stage a crepe bandage is best, as it has to come off again. Never use grease on the wound, as this will make it impossible to stitch if that is necessary. Jagged wounds that are over an inch (2.5cm) long normally require stitching.

After treating the wound, the vet will bandage it up as needed. Nowadays there are some excellent self- sticking bandages that mould to the horse's leg. Not only do they hold the dressing in place; they also support the leg. Covering wounds that are not on the leg is not so easy, but there your surgeon will decide how best to do it. Once you have been shown what to do, follow the vet's instructions.

Puncture Wounds

A puncture wound is a hole. These are the most serious of all wounds, regardless of size, because as soon as the wound's cause is removed – a nail, a prong, any object that is longer than it is wide – the skin starts to heal and close over, while the wound festers underneath. It is for this reason that puncture wounds are discouraged from closing until the internal part has fully healed. The sole and the heel are the places that most commonly sustain puncture wounds (*see* Feet, page 111), but other sites can be damaged too.

Call for veterinary help as soon as there is any sign of a puncture wound, regardless of size, as antibiotics are essential to prevent infection; then poultice.

Small puncture wounds are often missed, for unless the hair is clipped away they are not always noticeable unless they start to seep. Then they appear as a damp patch. On finding a puncture wound, clip the area with clippers, using first the coarse blade, then the medium, and finally the fine, to clear the site so that it can be seen; otherwise it will 'vanish' again. If the horse is already clipped, you can use just the fine blade. In some places where it is too awkward to clip, you may need to use round-nosed, curved-blade scissors, but the clippers will give a smoother surface and the coat will regrow more neatly.

To ensure that puncture wounds do not go unnoticed, run your hand over the skin – body, legs and head – each day; and if you feel a scab, inspect it. Puncture wounds will be sore, probably swelling if they have been there for a while, and the pus seeping out will be rather like a tiny molehill. If in doubt, do not waste time. They can be very deep.

Friction Wounds

These are caused by ill-fitting tack, saddles, bridles and rollers, not to mention boots, bad bandaging, and New Zealand rugs left on day after day without being changed or readjusted. The skin is rubbed repeatedly until in the end the surface is rubbed off, leaving a very sore area. If it is not treated and the cause dealt with, the wound will get worse and eventually become poisoned. The affected area should be washed thoroughly using pure soap, and then antiseptic cream or spray applied, depending on where it is. Sores on the back need to be healed and then, if necessary, hardened with surgical spirit. Mouths too, can suffer wounds from ill-fitting bits and

Trotting up a horse, lame in front.

Trotting up a horse, lame behind.

*Testing the degree of extension
in the forelimb.*

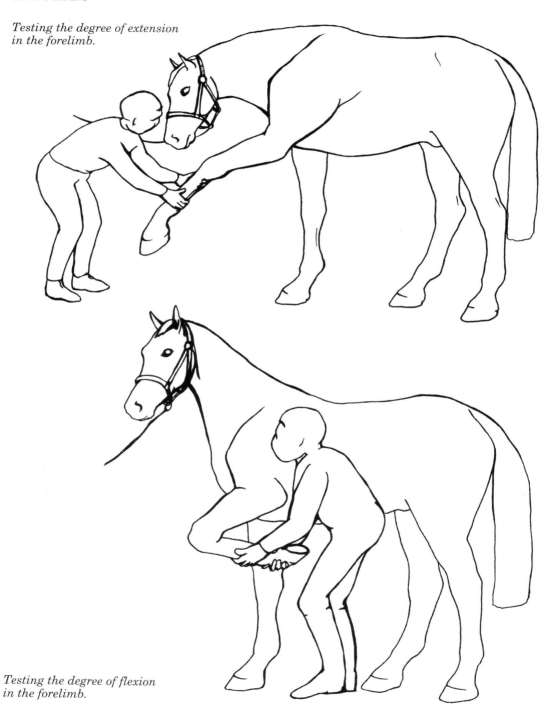

*Testing the degree of flexion
in the forelimb.*

rough handling. These sores are the owner's fault in nine cases out of ten. If the saddle is causing a problem, have the horse's back checked by a chiropractor or physiotherapist to ensure that there is no misalignment of the spine, withers, hips, shoulders or the axis of the neck; misalignment can lead to problems under the saddle, although in many cases the saddle is responsible for causing the misalignment in the first place. Choose a qualified person that has a really good record.

SWELLING

Swelling indicates inflammation, which is characterized by heat. Swelling may occur with a number of injuries, or through bruising or poisoning, or through strain. To reduce or inhibit swelling, the temperature of the affected area must be reduced, so the immediate treatment is cooling. For the first twenty-four to forty-eight hours use a cold-water hose and a cooling pack – if you haven't one of the proprietary cooling packs that are now available, a pack of frozen peas will work. In the old days one applied gamgee soaked in cold water, the heat in the leg promptly dried the dressing out. Ice keeps it cold longer. After the cooling spell, turn to poulticing. If bandaging ice onto the leg, cover first with gauze to make it as comfortable as possible and to stop the hair sticking to it.

COMMON INJURIES

Strains

This means a pulled tendon or ligament, which will require resting for some time. Quick action can help. The quicker the action the greater the likelihood that the horse will make a full recovery. Cold treatment, as described above, should be applied immediately, but call for help.

Nowadays, scanners can detect the source of the strain very well, which makes things easier. Portable X-rays are also available, and if your vet does not have one, a colleague will, no doubt, help

The first turn-out after box rest is always an anxious moment. River Gipsy, April 1994.

out. River Gipsy had an old swelling on the front of her off hind leg for some time, but no one could determine the cause. A portable X-ray machine was brought to her, and she was X-rayed. The results were clear. Since she had a long stride, I wondered if she was knocking the joint with her forefoot, so I put Yorkshire boots on. To my surprise it worked, and the bulk of the swelling went.

Tendon injuries need supporting and must be bandaged with a support bandage over gamgee. Tendons are bandaged between the knee and the fetlock. The tension and pressure must be kept even. Use clean bandages every day, otherwise the tension will be wrong: wash, dry and roll the bandages up tight before applying. Strained tendons must be re-bandaged at least twice a day – three to four times in some cases. Galavant's treatment involved re-bandaging eight times a day, but it was worth it. Rest is always essential, and should continue for weeks rather than days, depending on what your surgeon decides and the course of treatment. Whatever the instructions, follow them to the end; do not give up.

Skinned Limbs

As a youngster, River Gipsy had the hair and skin on her hind legs damaged from stifle to coronet. This kind of injury most commonly results from a horse's becoming entangled in wire. She was healed by being bathed three times a day with warm, weak antiseptic, and then covered with warmed zinc and castor oil cream. It was very sore. And the little mare was very good. While she ate from her feed bucket on the floor, I held the rope in one hand and bathed the extensive wounds with the other hand for about ten to fifteen minutes at a time, then gently smoothed the whole area with warm cream (she would not tolerate it cold).

After about two months the hair was back, unaltered. I had to trim her tail up to her hocks to keep it out of the way of the cuts. Hard though it may be to cut a tail short, they do grow again and if left they can cause problems, as they hold dirt.

Another horse a few months older than River Gipsy, had a similar accident. His tail was left long, and covered in dried blood and muck, as were his hind legs. He eventually healed, but he was badly scarred. He always would have been, as a section of flesh had been torn off, but it was made worse because the edges were allowed to crust and dry up, and form a lid. I think that wound powder had been used, as was common then, and in many cases probably is today. It seems to be the standard treatment on the shelves. All the same he grew into a very talented horse and that was the main thing. It really is essential though to wash the tail and any parts covered in blood or dirt after an accident, and thereafter keep them clean. Failure to do so either leads to more problems or prolongs the current one.

Overreaches

These are caused by the hind hoof striking the front leg or heel. Depending on the force of the strike, the injury may be a bruise, or it may be a cut, which may be only slight but can be deep, especially if the hind hoof treads on the heel and pins it. The back of the fetlock or even the tendon can be injured, too, normally when jumping. Heels require cleaning very thoroughly, and then poulticing. The heel is an awkward site, so I sew the poultice onto the gamgee to help prevent the dressing from slipping.

If the tendon has been cut get help straight away; the quicker it is seen the better the chance of saving it. Sadly some cannot be saved, and the tendon never heals sufficiently to let the horse work again.

Knees

These are normally cut by a fall, which not only cuts into the joint, but also causes a lot of bruising. A slight graze can usually be treated by the owner, but lacerated wounds will require professional attention to ensure that no damage has been done to the joint – a deep wound can release the joint fluid. Stitching is not possible, so they have to be treated as open wounds and healed from the bottom outwards, like any other similar wound, anywhere on the body. First clean by hosing, and, or, rinsing with antiseptic wash. Hosing will ease the bruising and stop the bleeding. At this stage it is essential to get the wound clean. If it is feasible, clip the hair off around it immediately, as the pain worsens as the numbness wears off and the horse will resent the attention.

Over the years I have had rather a lot of knees to heal. Points was my first, and she was the only one never to heal up level and with the correct hair colour – one knee finished with no hair and the other with white regrowth, which is sadly the norm for many horses. Powder was used on her knees, and I was told not to do anything else. When Willow Moth decided to accidentally trip up on the road, hitting a lump of mud, on the point of my selling her, I had no intention of letting her knees heal with a scar! The veterinary surgeon who came out, helped me clean them and remove the grit; then he gave me a special ointment that kept them soft and extracted the pus as it was produced. They healed without a mark. It was cleaned twice a day and re-dressed. It happened in November and by February I had sold her at an excellent profit – I had earned every farthing. When we bought her as a rescue case, we had to have an iceberg-like wart removed from above her eye, this too, though stitched, ended up with hardly a scar. I believe the same ointment was used once the stitches were out.

Galavant was my next knee injury, she slipped during schooling over walls, and seemed fine, but at the next failed to bend her leg and hung upside down over the wall before falling. We used a poultice to reduce the swelling caused by bruising, and extracted the dirt, thereby preventing infection. First we had to clean the knees very carefully and thoroughly. I then put a long piece of Tubigrip on over the leg and well up above the knee. Inside this I placed the prepared poultice, turned down the top half of the Tubigrip over the gamgee, then bandaged the leg up from below the knee to the fetlock. (To hold the gamgee in place while you turn the tubigrip down, it helps to use a short length of plaster just to lock the edges.) I found this worked extremely well: Galavant could lie down and the poultice stayed in place.

Poultice for about forty-eight hours or for however long your veterinary surgeon advises. Then, after cleaning the wound each day, apply whatever ointment has been prescribed. The wound must heal from the inside to prevent infection being trapped, so ten days after the injury I poultice for twenty-four to forty-eight hours to draw out any lingering poison and allow healing to progress properly. If it was not done at the outset, clip the hair off as soon as possible to ensure that no granules form around the edge of the wound and get stuck in the hair. Each day you should find the centre getting smaller and smaller as the wound heals and the depth slowly rises to normal level, looking clean and healthy. If during this progress there are any signs of seeping or yellowing, poultice again for twenty-four hours, just to make sure that all is well. If in doubt, telephone your vet for further advice. By the time the centre of the wound closes, the hair should be returning normally.

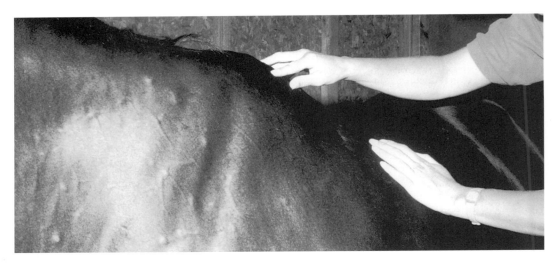

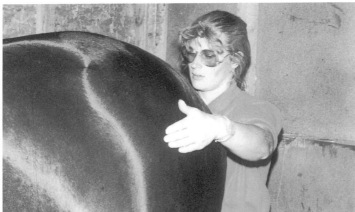

(Above) *Sore muscles and skeletal misalignments may hinder a full recovery from other injuries. Isobel Prestwich checking River Gipsy in July 1991.*

(Left) *Isobel Prestwich checking the alignment of River Gipsy's pelvis prior to manipulation.*

Chiropractic manipulation of the sacroiliac joint.

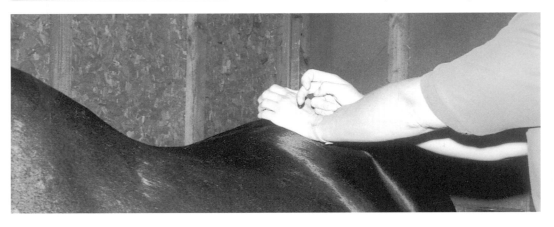

Back Problems

These occur in many horses. They may cause the horse either to be reluctant to work really well, or to move unevenly. Yet back problems often go undiagnosed because the owner does not investigate the possibility that back pain is causing the symptoms. Such horses will benefit from the attention of a fully qualified and experienced chiropractor, physiotherapist or osteopath, many of whom also treat humans. If you do use one, and you want to claim the fees on your insurance, your veterinary surgeon must approve of the chosen practitioner because the claim must be acknowledged by your vet.

Feet

Even well-cared-for feet are occasionally injured. It is easy to tread on a nail or have a shoe slip so that the nail goes into the foot causing a puncture wound (*see* page 104). Extract the nail, and then poultice, fixing the dressing with a poultice boot. If you do not have a poultice boot, you can strap the dressing onto the sole and then pad it with gamgee, before putting strong plastic over the whole hoof and securing it. Some holes will need to be cut open, especially if an abscess should crop up. Once open it must be poulticed before packing with either Stockholm tar or a mixture of Stockholm tar and fibre flour to make a paste. This is excellent under a shoe. As with all puncture wounds, you should carry out treatment under instruction from your vet.

Corns can also affect the horse's feet. Persistent corns must be surgically cut out, and the remaining hole can be fairly large. For these cases, special shoes are often required until healed.

Bruising to the foot may occur when stones become jammed in against the frog. First remove the cause of the bruising and

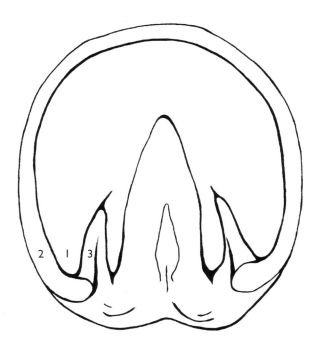

The horse's foot showing the seat of corn (1); between the heel (2); and the bar of the foot (3).

then hose to prevent swelling and to stem any bleeding. The foot should then be soaked in a warm antibiotic wash, or warm saline solution, to which Epsom salts have been added, and then poulticed. Tubbing in this manner before poulticing can help to prevent or draw out abscesses.

Eyes

Both infections and injuries can affect the eye, and in most cases you will be pre- scribed either an ointment or some drops.

To apply either, carefully open the eye and squeeze the ointment or drops along the lower line.

Eye problems can be tricky, but if you refuse to give up and keep on treating the problem you have a good chance of suc- cess. Eye ulcers, from which River Gipsy suffered, cause the eyes to cloud over In her case, the off-side eye, once cleared, stayed clear; but the nearside eye became susceptible to anything – knocks, stray eyelashes – and it was hard to know what would happen next, but I did retain her sight.

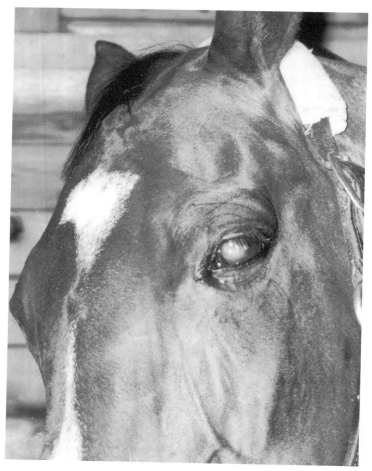

River Gispy's keratitis: the result of an eyelash turning in towards the eyeball.

10 Ailments and Diseases ―――――――――

A horse may become ill for a number of reasons. Viruses will cause a variety of diseases; wounds and injuries may result in infection or secondary disease; accidents, such as poisoning, can cause symptoms that range from the relatively mild to the severe; and poor husbandry can give rise to numerous conditions.

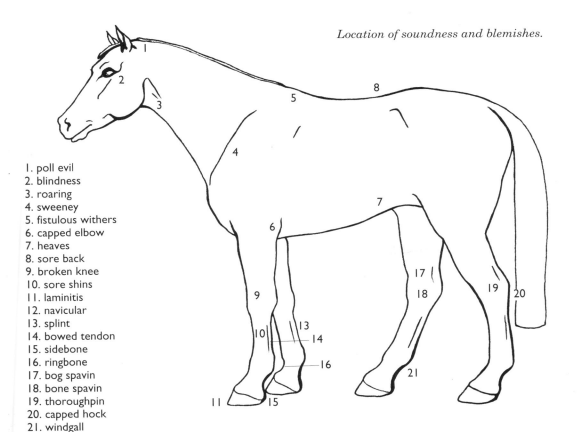

Location of soundness and blemishes.

1. poll evil
2. blindness
3. roaring
4. sweeney
5. fistulous withers
6. capped elbow
7. heaves
8. sore back
9. broken knee
10. sore shins
11. laminitis
12. navicular
13. splint
14. bowed tendon
15. sidebone
16. ringbone
17. bog spavin
18. bone spavin
19. thoroughpin
20. capped hock
21. windgall

COLDS AND INFLUENZA

These are caused by viruses. Influenza is an acute disease of the respiratory tract causing coughing, a high temperature and muscular stiffness, as well as running eyes and nose, and sometimes shivering, although the symptoms may range from mild to severe. The pulse and breathing rates may rise, and the horse may also show a lack of appetite. If you suspect your horse has flu, call the vet. While the horse is undergoing treatment (which may include antibiotics to combat complications caused by bacteria) it is essential to keep the patient in a warm, well-ventilated (but draught-free) box. Pneumonia may develop as a secondary condition, and damage to the heart may also occur. In these cases, the patient will probably need to visit a specialist veterinary surgery or equine hospital. In any case, a horse with flu should be fully rested for at least six weeks. Equine influenza can be prevented by vaccination (*see* Chapter 4).

Colds, which are characterized by a runny nose and eyes, are not so serious, but they should nevertheless be treated with respect. Your vet may give you instructions over the telephone, but if your horse has a high temperature, or there are any signs that the condition may be flu, he will come to examine the horse and give any treatment required.

For the horse with a cold or influenza, mashes are the easiest food to swallow. Do not give any hard food. It is important to allow time for the horse to convalesce, so do not ride until your vet indicates that a full recovery has been achieved.

It is worth pointing out here that in some cases horses may initially appear to be suffering from a viral infection but are then found to have some form of cancer. Since cancer is not easily detected, it may not be discovered until the patient is beyond treatment.

COUGHS

Coughs are caused by a variety of agents, both bacterial and viral, and are symptomatic of a number of conditions, including influenza (*see* above). Allergy to moulds will cause coughing, most especially in a condi-

For the treatment of respiratory disease, a variety of powders may need to be added to the horse's short feed on a daily basis.

Injections

Owners do not normally give injections. Any necessary drugs are supplied in the form of paste, powders or granules, which are either put in the feed or administered with an oral syringe. However, in some cases, owners will be given permission to give injections once the vet is satisfied that they are reliable and capable. Over the years, I have given a vast number. On the first occasion I was nervous about doing it, but I plucked up the courage and did a competent job. At that time, syringes and needles had to be cleaned by the user using surgical spirit; nowadays, one is given a sterile syringe and disposable needles which makes it far easier. Some years later I was obliged to start giving injections again after River Gipsy was vandalized with the shotgun. When the pellets started to erupt from the skin, causing infection, she was prescribed tranquillizers to combat the pain. These were to be administered by intramuscular injection on a regular basis, and since the vet had to travel from twenty miles away each time it was decided that I should administer them myself. I always used her hindquarters, and she was remarkably good, never once made a fuss. Later she also had to have endless injections of penicillin, which needed a large needle, and a vast amount of fluid.

Giving an injection

1. Select an injection site – your vet will advise you on the best locations. I always use the hindquarters, but you must watch that you do not get kicked. Do not give injections in the neck: this area contains many delicate structures, and only a qualified vet can inject there.

2. Clean the area with antiseptic applied with cotton wool.

3. If the syringe is not already charged, fill it. Pull the handle out, push the needle into the bottle, which is upside down to keep air off the top, and push the handle in to discharge the air. Then draw the required amount of the liquid into the syringe, and extract. Keep the dose absolutely as prescribed; never alter it.

4. Once the syringe is filled, place the bottle in a safe place. Point the syringe upwards and discharge a fraction of the liquid from the needle to ensure that there is no air in the syringe. Remove the needle carefully from the syringe and hold it between your first finger and thumb, pointing downwards.

5. With the bottom edge of your hand, thump the injection site two or three times. Immediately follow this with the needle. Push it straight in.

6. With the needle inserted, attach the syringe, which has been held safely in the other hand. Check that no blood flows back into the needle. If it does you will have to start again with a new injection site. If all is clear, gently push the handle down until the full dose has been injected into the muscle.

7. Extract the needle. Wipe away any fluid or blood that may come out, as it sometimes does. Hold a ball of cotton wool over the spot until the bleeding stops.

8. Wrap the syringe and needle up carefully. I always return them to the surgery. Safety is vital.

In the normal course of events, you should not have to give your horse any injections; but on rare occasions it may be necessary. Never give injections without sanction first.

tion called Small Airway Disease (SAD), which causes a build-up of mucus in the lungs. In such cases, good husbandry is all important. The horse should be kept in a dry, well-insulated but well-ventilated stable, with dust-free (not deep-litter) bedding (*see* Chapter 7). Hay must be absolutely dust free, so the vacuum-packed haylage is

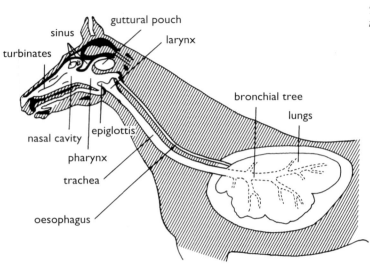

The component parts of the respiratory system.

Labels on diagram: sinus, guttural pouch, larynx, turbinates, bronchial tree, lungs, nasal cavity, epiglottis, pharynx, trachea, oesophagus

a good choice. Worm infestation will also cause coughing, and this should be avoided by regular worming (*see* Chapter 4).

STRANGLES

This is an acute, infectious, bacterial disease of the mucus membranes of the nasal passages and pharynx. It then infects the lymphatic gland, or the submaxillary gland, under the jaw, where it will cause an abscess to form, although it can also occur in other parts of the body. One indication of an infection is dark coloration of the normally salmon-pink membrane of the inner eye; another symptom is a high temperature. On one occasion, Castania had been in contact with a number of other horses, including her son Loyal Toast, prior to an outbreak of strangles. As soon as I saw the inside of her eye darkening, I called the veterinary surgeon, who came out and gave her some antibiotics. She recovered quickly and did not develop an abscess, but Loyal Toast was not so lucky and developed a very large one.

If an abscess does form under the upper jaw it needs to be poulticed to draw it out. First I bathed the area with a towel soaked in hot antiseptic solution and then wrung out. Then I made a poultice from lint and cotton wool – no gamgee in those days – and fixed it to the site by stitching it on to a Dutch foal headcollar. The headcollar was fitted as short and tight as possible to keep it close. It took about ten days to get it to burst; once it had my horse recovered fast. One can tell when the abscess is coming to bursting point by pressing the top with a finger – if it can be depressed easily then it is ripening. Once burst; clean everything up very carefully to ensure that none of the infected pus remains. Continue cleaning and dressing until healed.

ABSCESSES

Abscesses may result from strangles (*see* above), or through an infected injury, or as a result of inexpertly given injections, or from bacteria gaining access to the skin.

Strangles.

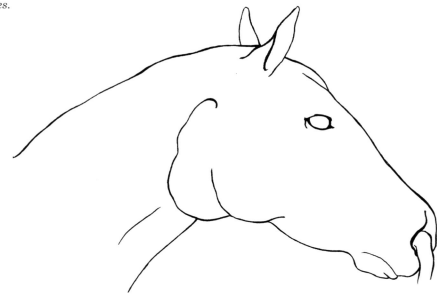

River Gipsy developed an abscess on her shoulder following her being shot with shotgun pellets. The infection migrated down her near fore leg, causing immense swelling and pain, and ended up blowing a hole out on her coronet, whence we started to poultice it to draw out all the filth and get back to normal. (This was only a year after her crashing fall on the road.) The pellets were now erupting. Her foot lost the outside of

Dehydration and Heat-stroke

Dehydration and heat stroke are serious conditions. Heat-stroke occurs during hot weather when there is insufficient shade and/or lack of water is the cause. The symptoms include a high temperature and rapid breathing, deepened hollows above the eyes, and pinched-looking nostrils, and dehydration. In a dehydrated animal the skin becomes hot and dry, and when pinched between finger and thumb it will remain raised on release rather than returning to normal.

Your immediate action on finding a horse with heat-stroke should be to remove him to a shaded area with plenty of ventilation and hose down him down, sponging the head with cold water. Ask for advice in case further help is required. If the horse starts to feel stress from the heat while you are out riding, take him home as quietly as pos-

sible, keeping in the shade where possible. Do not ride at the hottest time of the day, if avoidable.

Dehydration is loss of water from the tissues. It typically occurs when an animal suffers prolonged diarrhoea or is denied access to water to replace fluids. When I bought Galavant as a rescue case in August 1970, her condition was desperate. She was found with no sign of food and only a dredge of dirty water in a bucket. During hard frosts in winter, horses can suffer badly from a lack of water; some owners refuse to provide water at least three times a day, leaving their horses with only a frozen trough. As their bodies dry out from lack of fluid and intense cold, they become weaker and weaker. A horse can withstand starvation for quite some time, but he will not survive a lack of water for long.

the wall, so we used the half-shoes that have one section left out, normally on the inside but in this case on the outside, until the hoof had regrown sufficiently to enable the farrier to nail a full shoe on.

SKIN CONDITIONS

Skin problems may arise for a number of reasons. The most obvious things to affect the skin are insect bites and stings. For wasp stings, vinegar is the best tonic to apply, while bicarbonate of soda is an excellent remedy for bee stings. (These treatments work effectively on humans as well as animals.) However, should a horse or pony be stung in the mouth, or in numerous places by a swarm of bees or wasps, call your vet immediately. As with humans the horse can be in serious danger.

Ringworm

This is a contagious skin disease caused not by a worm but by a fungus, which produces greyish scabby areas with hair loss. However, it is not always easy for the layman to diagnose it. Depending on the specific cause, the lesions may or may not be itchy. Ringworm must be treated by your veterinary surgeon. The condition is transmissible to humans and other animals, so the animal should be kept isolated and you should be especially conscientious about washing and disinfecting your hands after contact.

Mud Fever

This is a very common illness that occurs in both horses and ponies during wet conditions. It is caused by a bacterium, which gains access to skin made tender by the grit in mud. It is one skin problem that can be checked with quick action, but if ignored it can become very serious and

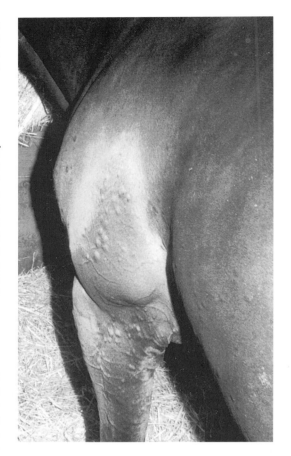

Gipsy's second bout of urticaria, an allergic response whose origin is often unknown.

take many months to cure. Cracked heels are a form of mud fever.

Check the heels every day by slipping your fingers over every inch of the heels, being very careful to feel under the fetlock and into the groove at the bottom of the pastern. If a scab is felt, do not ignore it. Clip off the hair. (Mud fever is in fact far easier to prevent if the heels are kept clipped throughout the winter.) Use coarse blades if no injuries are present; but if they are, clip first with coarse, then with medium and then with a fine blade. If you do not have clippers, use round-nosed, curved scissors. Now soften the scabs by bathing with antiseptic wash, or pure soap. Removing the scabs can be hard if they are established, but they must come off. A short clean brush can be used – at least I was told to use one once in a bad case. It does exacerbate the soreness, but the skin will be sore anyway and it is more important to ensure that the scabs are removed. In severe cases, it may be necessary to apply a poultice before trying to remove the scabs. Once you have cleared the area, dry it thoroughly with a piece of gamgee and then work an antiseptic ointment into the skin. In the past I have used antiseptic sprays, but they tend to form more scabs that are extremely hard to remove; this must be avoided at all costs because scabs protect the bacteria, allowing them to multiply underneath. Clean every day and re-treat. Do not return the horse to the paddock until the condition has been remedied.

Once mud fever has set in it can last a very long time, so in severe cases you must be prepared for a long haul. But do not give up. River Gipsy acquired it one year while in another yard, and it took us from January until June one year to cure it. Her fetlocks and heels had not been clipped that winter. Clipping enables you to wash the feet more easily, and to dry them more quickly, which is an important factor in preventing the condition. I first used clipping as a preventative measure with Galavant and Castania, clipping them to the top of the fetlock. The idea caught on and other people started doing it as they saw how effective it was. Most people use cold water to wash the feet, but I use warm water and some insecticide shampoo to get the skin really clean. In fact I had to bath Galavant after hunting as her skin reacted so badly to the mud and sweat, which if left to dry, set off mud fever, even on her stomach. Thorough washing and drying, and keeping her warm with rugs and bandages, solved the problem.

COLIC

Colic is a generic term meaning abdominal pain. It is not a disease but a disorder that arises through blockage or inefficient functioning of the gut. It affects the horse more than any other animal, and the symptoms may range from the relatively mild to the fatally severe. It can occur at any age. On one occasion, my five-month-old foal, Canyon, was found with colic; in his case it had resulted from eating grass whose protein content had been raised to a dangerous level through rapid growth following rain. Luckily Canyon recovered quickly after veterinary treatment. Following the attacks from vandals in her field, River Gipsy was very prone to colic but grew out of it; although grass sickness is colic-related, and we believe it was this that eventually killed her.

There are different types of colic, caused by a variety of problems in the gut, but there are a number of symptoms that should alert the vigilant owner to suspect the condition. Colic makes horses restive, and they will often paw the ground and break out in a sweat. Respiration may be shallow, and the pulse fast. If the bout of colic does not then subside, the horse may keep looking around at the stomach, on even try to kick at it. The horse may have an urge to roll. Constipation and difficulty staling are also signs of some types of colic. In some cases, the horse's gut may twist, in which case the prognosis is poor. Gentle walking sometimes helps to alleviate the symptoms, but a horse should not be forced to walk if he is very reluctant. He should be kept quiet, and allowed to lie down if he wishes. Food and water should be removed. If the symptoms have not abated within twenty minutes, call out a veterinary surgeon. Time counts.

Keep a close eye on the patient until the horse's condition is back to normal. If in any doubt, telephone the surgery. When the stomach has fully recovered and stabilized,

River Gipsy looking well, if a little bloated, on the day before she died.

the horse can be allowed a small bran mash and water. In some serious cases, surgery may be required to remove the cause of a blockage, which often entails a visit to a specialist hospital. Again, speed and time are vital.

GRASS SICKNESS

This very serious condition occurs during the summer months after a horse has been put out to grass. There are various theories about what causes it. Toxins, viral disease and stress have all been put forward as precipitating factors. There are various strains of the disease, and the symptoms vary with each, but it is almost

always fatal. The symptoms may come on suddenly, and death occur within a couple of days, or the horse may linger for some days or weeks, becoming progressively more listless and weak, with no interest in food. Latterly a discharge from the nostrils may appear, coupled with excessive salivation, difficulty in swallowing, shivering and constipation. The intestine may become impacted and the pain caused may induce the horse to roll. The horse becomes unmanageable and violent.

It is grass sickness that we believe killed River Gipsy. When I found her she was very drowsy, and just standing there with her head down and her nose running. She liked me stroking her but did not move. In addition to the normal droppings, there were

120

two piles of bright-green sludge, resembling cow-pats. She had clearly lain down at some point because her rug was stained with it, as were her hindquarters, tail, and even the walls of the box, but her bed was not unduly disturbed. When I had skipped out the night before, the only noticeable thing was that there were fewer droppings than usual. With hindsight the only other clue that all was not quite well was that although her appetite had been good, short feeds had not held much interest for her for some time. But since she was out at grass all day, this in itself did not seem suspicious. Her coat and general condition were good. Her stomach had been rather large since the incident when she was doped by vandals a couple of years previously, but once again that could have been put down to her age (she was nearly eighteen).

On discovering her condition, I went home to call the vet for help and advice, and then returned to her. Nothing had changed. I cleaned everything up, as advised, so that I could more easily determine any change. I had to work round her because she was unable to move, but I got the floor clean and all the wet bedding out. She was now having difficulty passing urine, although prior to this she was passing a lot, and since it was quite strong I had thought she was coming into season. While I was cleaning the box, she started to shiver. As time passed the shivering became more violent, and under her rugs she was dripping with sweat. It had been cold and wet, so she was wearing two light rugs. I took one off, leaving the other draped over her quarters to prevent chilling, and dried her off. Then I re-rugged her, and she started to settle down. I cleaned her nostrils and eyes so that I could see how she was progressing, then I took her temperature – 103.6°F (39.7°C).

Once I had cleaned everything up and felt sure that I could leave her for a short spell, I returned home to phone the surgery again. The vet came as soon as surgery was over, at 11.30 a.m., and in the mean time I visited her several times. She was still very ill, but she looked as though she had come through the worst. The vet gave her two injections and told me to starve her for twenty-four hours. It was no longer thought necessary for me to visit her every half hour, but I continued to do so. At lunchtime I noticed that she was resting her quarters on the wall. There was no other sign of change, but I was not happy. I straightened her bed out and went home.

Half an hour later there was still no change, but I had barely reached home again when my friend's daughter came to fetch me because Gipsy was now falling around the box. It was impossible to get into the box with her. She was far too upset and did not know what she was doing. I immediately called the vet again, but he was unable to get to her in time; though it made little difference for I knew that he could not have saved her: she had damaged her head too badly in falling about the box. Within minutes she had collapsed, falling against the back wall with her head buried in the banked-up straw. And a couple of rather violent minutes later, at 3 p.m., she was dead. On examination she was found to have a twisted gut, and her stomach was flooded with fluid.

Many horses died of similar illness during the summer of 1995. I am not absolutely certain that it was grass sickness, but most of the symptoms suggest that it was.

CHOKE

Choke is caused by an obstruction in the oesophagus, usually a piece of food, such as an apple or carrot. Sugar-beet nuts can be a dangerous product if they are not soaked for twelve hours before being fed, because they can quickly swell and cause a blockage, preventing further food from progressing down into the stomach and compounding the problem.

If the object has become jammed at the entrance of the ooesophagus, it may be possible to ease it out, having first gained access by pulling the tongue out of the side of the mouth, between the front and back teeth. However, in most cases the blockage will occur further down, out of reach, and the horse may not be aware of the problem until it begins to cause pain. The primary symptoms are distress and standing with his neck stretched out, while salivating profusely. The saliva may appear at the nostrils, when there is a risk of pneumonia caused by inhaling it.

Choke is a serious condition that can be fatal, and it demands immediate veterinary attention. If you suspect your horse has choke, avoid lifting the head, remove any food or liquid, and keep the horse as quiet and calm as possible until the vet arrives.

AZOTURIA

Azoturia – also called as Monday morning disease or setfast – is the cramping up of the hindquarters in a painful muscle spasm that causes the horse to stagger or even to fall over by buckling at the knees. It comes on suddenly, usually soon after the horse has begun exercise. The horse may be moving freely one moment and then the next the cramp will set in. There are various theories on why it occurs, but it is precipitated by sudden rest periods during which the horse is fed concentrates in excess of the amount demanded by the horse's work.

This condition is very serious and potentially fatal. If you are riding when the horse shows symptoms, dismount immediately, call your vet, and let your horse rest. In no circumstances should you attempt to move him as this will reduce any chances of recovery. The patient will need to be kept warm, and he should be taken home by box.

LAMINITIS

This is an inflammation of the laninae, which are the paper-like vertical structures within the hoof. The condition causes extreme pain and restricts movement. Horses suffering acute laminitis will stand on the back of their heels to relieve the pressure, so when the forefeet are primarily affected, the horse will transfer his weight to the hindquarters resulting in the characteristic laminitic stance. Eventually the hooves will change shape as the pedal bone rotates, and hoof wall will become ridged and curled up in front. In advanced cases, movement becomes impossible, and the horse may lie down and be disinclined to stand up.

The eyes are another sign: they appear dark red inside and the pupils are widely dilated. Respiration is rapid and the horse may sweat. The pulse is also very fast, although it may weaken as exhaustion progresses. The temperature may rise between two and five degrees and will

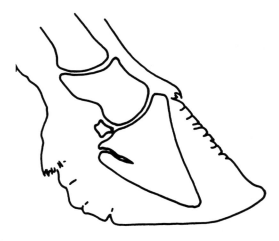

The laminitic foot, showing the rotation of the pedal bone, which occurs after separation of the horny and sensitive laminae in acute cases.

remain higher than normal throughout. One early sign is that the pumping of the artery behind the coronet become detectable. Place your centre finger on the artery and if there is a pronounced throb you may be able to take action before the feet become inflamed and more painful. In the early stages, the hoof and coronary band feel hot, although later on, as the laminae die off, the hoof will feel cooler than normal and only the coronary band will retain the heat.

These are not all the symptoms, but I think enough to warn an owner that help is required. Some people leave their horses with laminitis without treatment, but this is cruel and can only result in progressive deterioration. The main problem is to keep the patient in the stable with restricted, suitable food containing vitamins and minerals, as further rich eating will increase the suffering. Small, fat ponies are most commonly affected, though others may also suffer. Unfortunately once laminitis has been contracted (even if successfully treated), the patient will be prone to suffering in future.

If a laminitic horse lies down in the field and refuses to move, then the only course of action is to construct a temporary shelter around the horse. This can be done by surrounding the horse with straw bales over which you might place a board or sheet that is then secured to the bales. This is important because they must not be allowed to get cold. Get the patient into the stables as soon as possible. Cool the feet by hosing for about twenty minutes at a time, or soak them in a bowl of cold water if they can stand. They need professional help so call for it without delay. Only small feeds – mashes, and a little hay, or whatever you are advised to give – should be allowed until the horse has recovered. There are a number of causes of laminitis, but the most common one is the consumption of rich grass or excessive amounts of concentrate feeds. A sudden intake of excess carbohydrate causes bacterial changes and ultimately increased blood pressure, affecting the blood supply to the foot. A horse recovering from laminitis should be kept away from all grass until he is better; then he should be allowed access to poor, but clean, grazing for restricted spells.

NAVICULAR

This is an acute inflammation of the navicular bone and its associated structures inside the hoof. The front feet are the most prone to this horrid and painful disease, but in some cases, the hind feet can be affected too. In advanced cases, damage to the flexor tendon occurs.

Navicular is extremely painful, but since it progresses slowly it is difficult to diagnose in the early stages. The horse may leave the stable sound and then become lame, and vice versa, and these signs may be intermittent; but a typical early symptom is that of resting a foot in a forward, 'pointing' position. As the condition progresses, it may be noticed that the shoe on the affected foot is worn down at the toe. X-ray is the only reliable means of confirming navicular disease.

The cause of navicular is unknown, but concussion from work on hard ground is one possibility. Another theory suggests that the density of the bone may be altered by the absorption of toxins. This may occur during or after a serious illness, such as influenza or strangles, or an unnoticed cased of rheumatism. One school of thought connects navicular with serious viral infection or rheumatism. The possible link between strangles and navicular seems to be supported in the case of Castania's foal Loyal Toast, who contracted a serious bout of strangles at an early age and then, very sadly, at the age of six, suffered from navicular and had to be put down.

SWOLLEN LEGS

Several things may cause the legs to swell. Strains, wound infection and bruising are typical (*see* Chapter 9). Check carefully for any obvious causes, and rest if gentle walking does not reduce the swelling. Do not trot until the cause is known as this could result in further trouble. Over-feeding can cause swollen legs, so reduce the feeds for forty-eight hours and monitor progress regularly. If the heat does not subside seek professional help as the problem could be serious and require prompt attention.

SPLINTS

A splint is a bony enlargement that appears on the cannon bone following inflammation. In the early, inflamed stages the developing splint can cause severe lameness. Rest is required. In the old days the treatment was blistering, which involved burning off the unwanted extra bone. Castania had splints on both her front legs and the cracked hind leg following the accident in 1953. Splints are most frequently seen in young horses, though some older ones may develop a splint as a result of an injury. Veterinary treatment will be provided according to the severity of the splint. Some will disappear on their own, given time.

CURBS

Curbs are similar to splints, but they appear on the back of the hock, just above the tendon. In the early stages, they may cause lameness, which may continue if their precise location hampers the action of the joint. Seek advice. Curbs should not be confused with the bog spavin, which is a swelling caused by inflammation of the bone at the front of the hock joint, or the capped hock, which is swelling at the point of the hock.

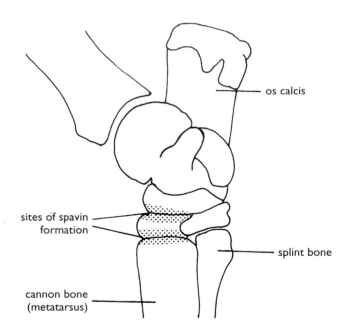

os calcis

sites of spavin
formation

splint bone

cannon bone
(metatarsus)

The hock.

Conclusion

In no way is *Nursing Your Horse* intended to cover every problem that you may come across. It is of course for the veterinary surgeon to decide how to treat an injury or illness. The aim of this book has been to help the owner to co-operate with the vet while enhancing the effects of treatment through good nursing.

No two horses are exactly the same, and since the effects of illness and injury are not always predictable it is impossible for a book to anticipate every eventuality. Nevertheless, the basic principles of sound nursing remain the same.

It is true that not all illnesses or injuries can be cured, and in some cases it will be impossible to save the patient. But there are also cases that might at first appear hopeless and yet are saved through prompt action and conscientious care. It is always worth putting in the extra time and effort to attend to the details, for it is often the little things that make the difference between ultimate success and failure.

It is becoming more and more apparent that animals are sensitive to their carer's state of mind, so always maintain a positive attitude. Caring, considerate nursing really can make a difference, so keep optimistic and do not give up.

A healthy horse is taken for granted. But one that fights back and recovers from serious illness or injury is something very special, and is in himself the greatest reward for your effort.

The author and River Gipsy, 1983, enjoying the rewards of patient nursing and attention to detail.

Index ——————————————————————